THE LEFTY'S SURVIVAL MANUAL

IF YOU HAVE EVER:

Developed blisters from cutting with
right-handed scissors,

Spilled sauce in a guest's lap because your
ladle's lip is on the outside,

Turned a lyrical love letter into abstract art
because your hand keeps smudging the
words that you have just written,

Opened your notebook, zealous to write,
and found an obtrusive lump of binding
where you would like to put your arm,

Made a glorious roast look like last month's
ground beef because the edge of your knife
was situated in the wrong place,

Known anyone who has ever experienced
one of these situations,

THEN THIS IS *YOUR* BOOK!

THE LEFTY'S SURVIVAL MANUAL

PETER NEIMAN
President, Aristera,
the Left Hand People™

Illustrated by Whitney Darrow

BANTAM BOOKS · TORONTO · NEW YORK · LONDON

As a service to our readers, Bantam has included in this book a catalog of products of interest to the left-handed person. All orders and inquiries should be directed to Aristera, The Left Hand People ®, 9 Rice's Lane, Westport, CT. 06880, who have guaranteed your satisfaction. See Peter Neiman's message on page 51.

THE LEFTY'S SURVIVAL MANUAL
A Bantam Book / March 1980

Book design by Kathleen Ferguson

ISBN 0-553-01225-8

Published simultaneously in the United States and Canada

Bantam Books are published by Bantam Books, Inc. Its trademark, consisting of the words "Bantam Books" and the portrayal of a bantam, is Registered in U.S. Patent and Trademark Office and in other countries. Marca Registrada. Bantam Books, Inc., 666 Fifth Avenue, New York, New York 10019.

PRINTED IN THE UNITED STATES OF AMERICA

0 9 8 7 6 5 4 3 2 1

CONTENTS

FOREWORD

Memo to: Professor Dexter, Psychology Department,
University Hall

Professor Sinister, Creative Arts Department,
University Hall

Dear Professors,

I need a couple of scientific bigwigs to write a foreword to our new book and catalog, to give it some tone. Both of you appear in it often, so I think you're naturals for the job.

How about it?

Best,

Peter B. Neiman
President
Aristera, the Left Hand People

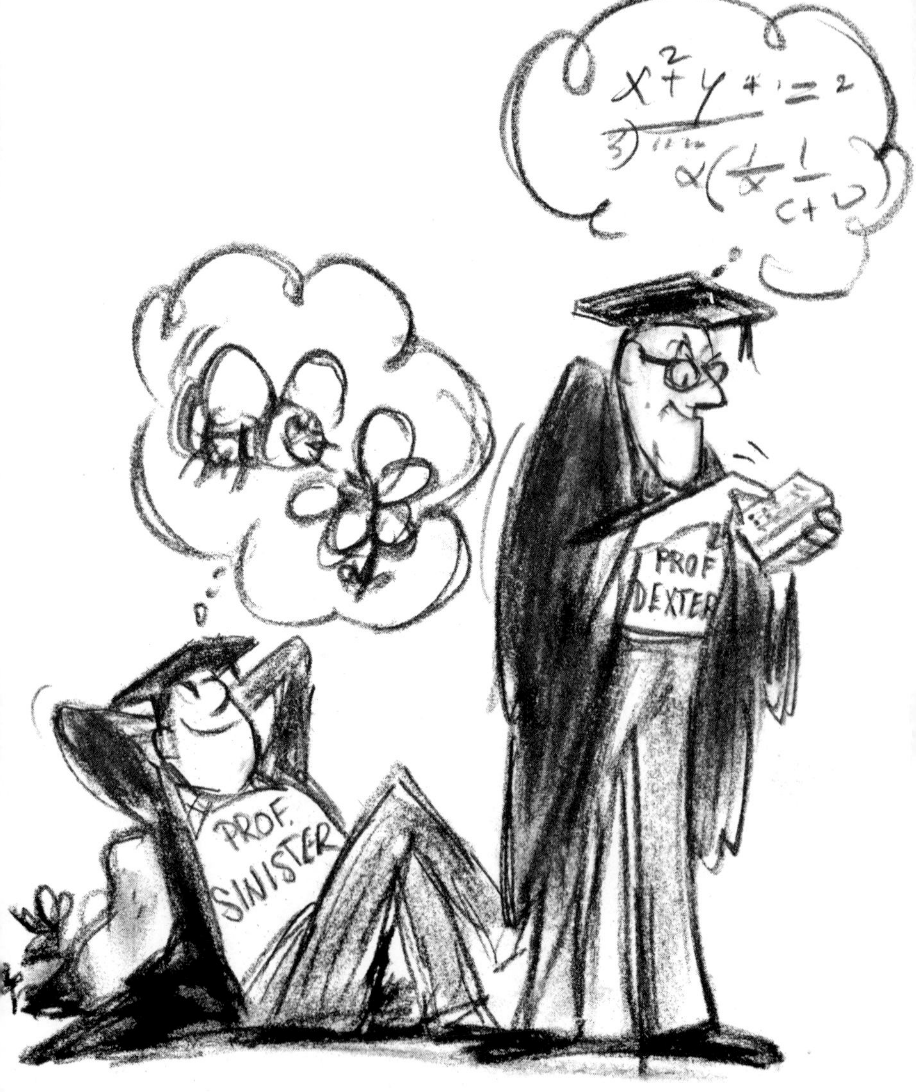
PROF. SINISTER
PROF DEXTER

Memo to: Peter B. Neiman, President, Aristera,
the Left Hand People

From: Professor Dexter

Dear Pete,

As a right-hander, I'm flattered that you mention my research here and there in your new book, and that you asked me to write a foreword to it.

I found the book to be amusing, educational, entertaining, informative, responsive to the needs of lefties, and useful. Notice that I listed these reasons in alphabetical order. It would also have been appropriate to have listed them in order of importance to me as a professor, i.e., educational, informative, responsive, entertaining, and amusing. I could have also taken the readers' point of view, which would have been amusing, useful, responsive, entertaining, informative, and educational.

Any way you look at it, it's a nice book, and good luck with it.

Right on!

Professor Dexter

Professor Dexter
Psychology Department

P.S. I notice you've also asked my left-handed colleague for a contribution. It won't be nearly as crisp and logical as mine; forgive him if he rambles.

cc: Professor Sinister, Creative Arts Department

Memo to: Peter B. Neiman, President, Aristera,
 the Left Hand People
From: Professor Sinister

Dear Pete,

I'm sure my esteemed colleague will present you with a well-organized foreword that will include at least one list. Dexter would be a whiz at classifying trees, but I'm sure he'd miss the beauty of the forest. My way is to look at the forest first, and then deal with classifying the trees (if I have to).

For example, your book conveys an image, a tone, a feeling about us lefties that can't be analyzed or compartmentalized by logic alone. Many of your readers will recognize this about themselves when they finish the *Survival Manual*, and will feel better about themselves as a result of it.

I see that you never mention one of us without the other. Dexter and I are extremes; everyone has a piece of us both, and it takes both of us to hold a pointer to the truth.

I could go on, but I don't want to be accused of rambling.

Left on!

Professor Sinister

Professor Sinister
Creative Arts Department

cc: Professor Dexter, Psychology Department

INTRODUCTION

Statistically speaking, left-handed people have more physical and behavioral problems in the first five years of their lives. They also often grow up to become creative geniuses.

As well as stubborn, rebellious, clumsy in some circumstances, and amazing-graceful in others.

They have been consistently put down, almost everywhere, from the beginning of recorded time, and have contributed just as consistently to artistic, social, and scientific progress, way out of proportion to their small numbers.

Fortunately for their sakes, lefties generally possess a good sense of humor and an exuberantly healthy ego. There is little false modesty among left-handed people.

This is a book dedicated to them. Some of the questions we address are:

- What is a lefty? (The answer is more complicated than you might think.)
- How does the world look at lefties as being "different"? How much of it is real, and how much is information based on biased tests, created by right-handed testers?
- How do the new discoveries about the workings of our brain relate to lefties?
- Why is it important to raise *everyone's* consciousness about the special nature of lefties?
- Can specially designed tools and equipment really make life easier for lefties?
- What to do if you are left-handed,
  Or are married to one,
  Or are the parent of one?
  Or, if you love one.
- How to order special products if you are a lefty,

A Note from Aristera:

We at Aristera operate a business servicing the needs of lefties through mail order.

The information contained in *The Lefty's Survival Manual* is based on our own extensive research, plus discussions with specialists and our experiences with the most expert group of all: our customers.

Every observation, fact, or number in the book is taken from our own experiences or from one of the books and articles you will find listed in the bibliography. Most of this material can be found in your local library; all of the books can be ordered directly from Aristera. If you have any questions at all, don't hesitate to let us know.

Enjoy!

WHAT IS A LEFTY?

Here's a simple quiz to get us started:

Q: Righties are people who do most things with their right hand.
   Yes or No?

A: Yes.

Q: Lefties are people who do most things with their left hand.
   Yes or No?

A: Maybe yes, Maybe no.

The catch here is that lefties don't fall neatly into one clearly defined category (actually, righties don't either). It would be a better idea to set up six groups to distinguish the people who:

1. Do practically everything with the right hand and almost never use the left hand.

2. Do most things with the right hand. They can use the left hand but favor the right one.

3. Can do almost everything equally well with either hand.

1

4. Do some things with the left hand and some with the right
   a. knowing in advance which hand they will use.
   b. not knowing in advance which hand they will use.
5. Do most things with the left hand. They can use the right hand but prefer the left.
6. Do practically everything with the left hand and almost never use the right hand.

Let's look at these groups in a diagram.

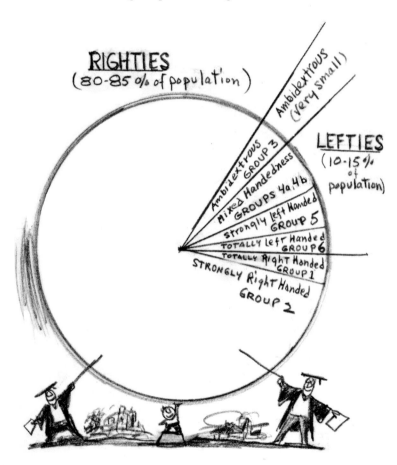

RIGHTIES
(80-85 % of population)

Ambidextrous
(very small)

LEFTIES
(10-15 %
of
population)

Ambidextrous
GROUP 3

Mixed Handedness
GROUPS 4a 4b

Strongly left Handed
GROUP 5

TOTALLY left Handed
GROUP 6

TOTALLY Right Handed
GROUP 1

STRONGLY Right Handed
GROUP 2

Groups 1 and 2 are righties and make up about 90 percent of the population (with group 2 having far and away the biggest share). The people who belong in group 3 are ambidextrous and are a very small percentage of the population. Most people who think of themselves as ambidextrous belong in group 4, people with mixed-handedness. Most lefties fall into group 4, and most of those into group 4a. People in subgroup 4b, confused dominance, can feel pretty miserable at times and, well, confused. Group 5 is the next biggest group of lefties. Group 6, like its righty counterpart, group 1, is extremely rare. Which group are you in?

As we proceed through *The Lefty's Survival Manual*, some readers will look at a section and think, "That's me! How did they know that?" Others will look at that same section and think, "Who are they talking about?" To use an analogy, if you thought of all people as ice cream, you could say that they all had some characteristics in common: cool, creamy, refreshing. Lefties would come in many flavors: chocolate, strawberry, butter pecan, pistachio. Most righties are plain vanilla.

The word *handedness* is not entirely accurate; the more general term *sidedness* is more appropriate, since most people have not only a preferred hand but also a preferred eye, ear, and foot. When these aspects of sidedness are not the same—e.g., a left-handed, left-eyed, right-footed person—some clumsiness and unhappiness can be the result.

Some common tasks that vary in handedness are:

Eating	Throwing
Writing	Holding your partner while making love
Brushing your teeth	Kicking
Using tools, i.e., a hammer	Swinging a bat, racket, or golf club

Using twist-off caps
Bathroom hygiene
Cutting with scissors
Stroking a pet

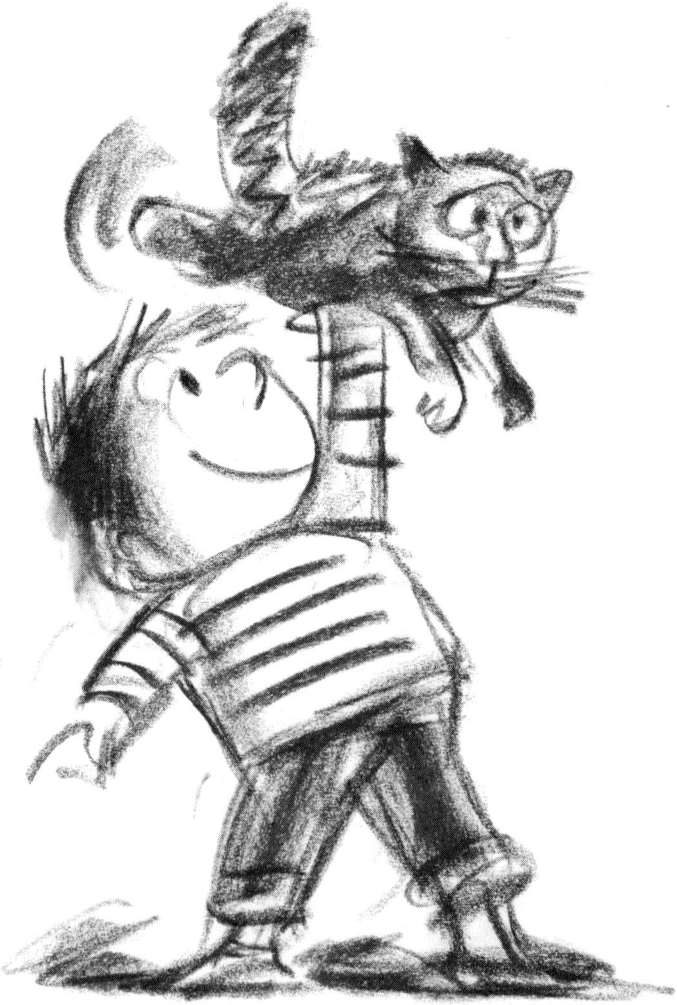

Our customers often tell us they were taught to do certain tasks, like writing, right-handed, but use their left hand for tasks and skills that were self-taught, like throwing a baseball.

The sequence in which we perform certain acts is another indication of sidedness: which shoe we put on first for example, or which arm goes into a shirtsleeve. Strong feelings are often involved in this example of sidedness: putting the "wrong" shoe on first can bring "bad luck" and spoil a day.

But we're still not telling the whole story. So far, we have been using "sidedness" to describe motor activity, the use of muscles, appendages, and organs to perform tasks and receive data. When we perform mental tasks, such as analytical reasoning, using language, recognizing patterns, imagining, guessing on hunches, making decisions, we also "choose sides." Being left- or right-handed is not just how you handle things but how you think and handle life.

ABOUT
YOUR BRAINS

Don't panic. This isn't heavy stuff, none of those anatomy diagrams that look like eggs scrambled with worms. We're just going to give you some facts you will find either fascinating or boring. (Depending on your brain!)

The human brain is really two half brains; sometimes referred to as the left and right hemispheres, which have different functions but work closely together. Here are some of these functions:

- Control of body movements, such as walking, grasping, moving lips and tongue to eat or talk.
- Sensing information delivered to the brain by eyes and ears.
- Thinking logically.
- Forming words in your brain in preparation for speaking or writing.
- Analyzing patterns and images, to recognize faces, for instance.
- Appreciating and producing music.

The first two items on the list: body movement and sensing information, are generally performed by both hemispheres, but done on behalf of different sides or parts of the body. For example, the left hemisphere controls

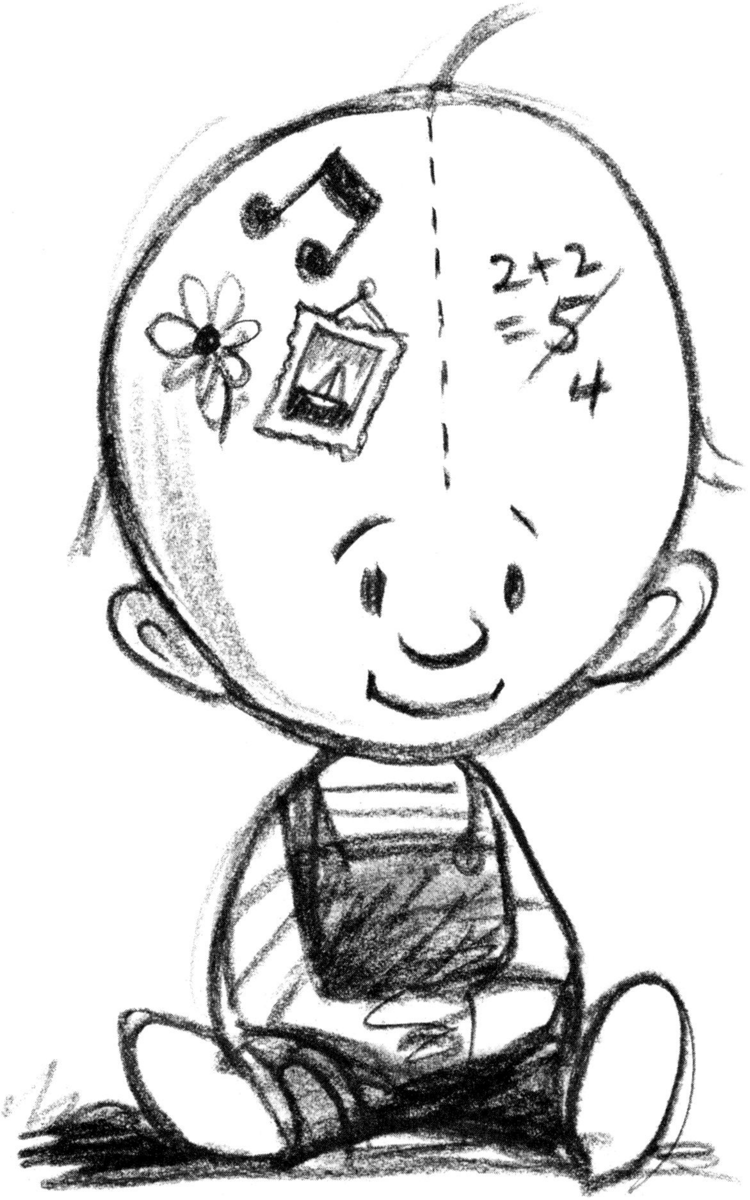
2+2
=5
4

movement of your right hand. The right hemisphere controls movement of your left. (Why these functions are criss-crossed, nobody yet knows.) The two hemispheres have to work cooperatively or else you couldn't do things like walking a straight line. (Certain kinds of brain damage can really mess up coordination for that reason.)

The situation is quite different for the remaining items on the list. They are generally *not* done in both hemispheres, but are assigned individually to one hemisphere or the other. Logical thinking, for example, will be done in just one half. That same half generally also does analytical processing and is the place where words are formed mentally. Pattern recognition, on the other hand, is done in the opposite hemisphere. So is music behavior.

Righties have a pretty consistent brain organization. The left half controls right hand movement and is also assigned logic, analysis and language. The right half controls pattern recognition, imagery, and musical ability, as well as the left hand. Since, for righties, the right hand lords it over the left, the hemisphere that controls it is often referred to as the "dominant" one, and the other one then gets called "sub-dominant." For right-handers the sub-dominant hemisphere is often thought of as the "dark" or silent hemisphere; the dreamier, more intuitive one.

Lefties are not nearly as consistent. All of them have brain reversal for hand dominance, but only about 45 percent also reverse all other functions. The other 55 percent reverse some but not others, which makes for a lot of colorful variety.

When we switch from one mental task to another, we also switch hemispheres, to some extent. That's one explanation why some people who stutter badly can sing the same words faultlessly, because they are switching control from the speech half to the music half.

The two hemispheres have very different ways of solving problems and most people "prefer" one side to the other. The dominant hemisphere (left for righties) likes to look at things logically, taking one step at a time. It would think like this: If all lefties are good guys and if Professor Sinister is a lefty, then it follows that Professor Sinister is a good guy.

The other hemisphere likes to solve problems holistically, looking at all the factors at the same time and coming up with an "intuitive" answer. Keep in mind that language—the ability to articulate one's thoughts—does not reside in this hemisphere. This is the "silent" hemisphere, which is why when people solve a problem its way, they have trouble telling anybody how or why they did it. Naturally, it is harder for me to articulate an example. I can come close by reminding you of an old poem by Thomas Brown that goes:

> *I do not love thee, Dr. Fell;*
> *The reason why, I cannot tell,*
> *But this I know, and know full well,*
> *I do not love thee, Dr. Fell.*

The poet knew what he knew, even though he couldn't explain it.

There is a test you can give people to find out which hemisphere they "prefer" for problem solving. Interpreting the test is fairly straightforward to righties but trickier for lefties, for reasons we'll see later. When presented with a simple, unemotional problem, most people tend to look upward toward the left or toward the right. The direction of the glance is always the opposite of the brain hemisphere that is doing the thinking at that moment. Here is the test:

Look your subject in the eye and ask him to tell you how many letters are in the word *Mississippi*. If he gazes to the right, he's using his left hemisphere; if he gazes to the left, he's using his right one.*

For righties, it's pretty safe to conclude that a gaze to the right means the person prefers to think with the left (logical) brain. You might think that lefties would test out consistently as just the reverse: that a gaze to the left would mean that their right (logical for them) brain is the problem-solver. Not so! Lefties' brains are not nearly as neatly compartmentalized as righties'. Remember, we said some functions are switched, some are not. Lefties do a lot more sharing of mental function between the two hemispheres, often producing more creative, unusual solutions.

There are fascinating implications for business, government, and society in the realization that people solve problems differently depending on their "sidedness." Someday, a better understanding of sidedness will be able to point a person to a truly satisfying life's work. The skills of a potter, for example, are primarily holistic, while those of a lawyer are primarily logical and analytical. This field of study is still young, and we'll be reporting new findings through customer bulletins and future editions of the Manual as fast as we hear about them.

*By the way, I've found that the test doesn't always work. Remember, the problem has to be unemotional. Some people are suspicious and think there's some kind of catch, or that I'm going to sneak up and tickle them while they're not looking. Getting emotional messes up the test results.

FAMOUS LEFTIES

(and what they have to say)

Great Scott! How do we handle this chapter? Make a list of all the famous people who ever lived, and then run a pencil through the occasional right-hander who snuck in? That's not really fair. What we'll do instead is list a few examples and put them into categories to please Professor Dexter. If your favorite famous lefty is left out, please don't scold us, but let us know.

I. Far Past

Rameses
Alexander the Great
Julius Caesar
Leonardo da Vinci
Michelangelo
Napoleon
Thomas Carlyle
Benjamin Franklin
Charles Lamb
Billy the Kid

II. Recent Past

Charlie Chaplin
Harry Truman
Pablo Picasso
John Dillinger
Harpo Marx
Marilyn Monroe
Clarence Darrow
Cole Porter
Nelson Rockefeller
Babe Ruth
Boston Strangler

III. Contemporary Scene

Prince Charles
Jimmy Connors
Gerald Ford
Whitey Ford
Paul McCartney
Ken Stabler
Reggie Jackson
Goldie Hawn
Bob Dylan
Danny Kaye
Carol Burnett
Pele
Yogi Berra
Robert Redford
Willis Reed
James Michener
Wally Schirra
Martina Navratilova
Ringo Starr
Ray Milland
Richard Dreyfuss
Professor Sinister

We have a similar problem with lefties' quotes, so we've just picked a few in three categories:

A. Quotes about left-handedness

Casey Stengel said: "Left-handers have much more enthusiasm for life. They sleep on the wrong side of the bed, and their heads become stagnant on that side." Thomas Carlyle, a nineteenth-century Scottish essayist and historian, was forced to become left-handed through an accident. The adjustment problems he experienced prompted him to remark: "Right-handedness is perhaps the very oldest institution."

The most eloquent and poignant quote by a lefty about left-handedness is the letter that Benjamin Franklin wrote (to anyone who would listen) on behalf of his left hand,

purporting to be from his left hand. It said, in part: "From my infancy I have been led to consider my sister [his right hand] as a being of a more educated rank. I was suffered to grow up without the least instruction, while nothing was spared in her education. She had masters to teach her writing, drawing, music, and other accomplishments, but if by chance I touched a pencil, a pen or a needle, I was bitterly rebuked; and more than once beaten for being awkward, and wanting a graceful manner.

(signed) The Left Hand"

B. Quotes that illustrate facts about your brains

When the two hemispheres of the brain conflict with each other for control of the body, they can get in each other's way. Scholarly books have been written on this subject, but Yogi Berra summed it all up: "You can't think and hit at the same time." Michelangelo understood where his real skill lay when he remarked: "A man paints with his brains, not his hands."

C. Quotes that just tickled us pink

Charles Lamb, nineteenth-century English essayist and critic, said: "There is nothing so nice as doing good by stealth, and being found out by accident." Edgar Guest had a two-line poem that also expressed this lovely thought:

The only deeds he ever hid
Were the acts of kindness that he did.

And finally, we've always enjoyed: "I never give them hell. I just tell the truth, and they think it's hell." Who else but Harry Truman could say that? Atta boy, Harry!

WHEN LEFTIES SHINE

In our opinion, the left-handed minority has always had an unusually high number of superachievers in all areas, compared to the population at large. Of course, you could say that about many other minorities as well. It's interesting to speculate on why this is so. Our own theory is that people excel when they are hit by challenge or adversity. Lefties have had to face a definite but not overwhelming amount of adversity—just enough to give many of them an extra measure of patience, fortitude, independence, emotional balance, and humor—helpful in overcoming some of the nonsense they have to put up with in this right-handed world.

Enough speculation. Here are some hard facts that say that lefties often have a unique competitive edge. As with most other aspects of left-handedness, there is not just one reason for this, but at least four different reasons why they shine:

1. *Because the task is inherently done better left-handed.* Bowling, for example. The spin imparted to the ball to make it curve into the strike pocket is counterclockwise and uncomfortable to a righty but is clockwise and familiar to a lefty, who has been conditioned to it from driving screws, turning door knobs, etc.

Typewriters are made with the most frequently used keys and operating controls on the left.

In baseball, the southpaw batter is nearer first base, the southpaw first baseman can better cover the field, and the southpaw pitcher can keep a better eye on first.

Beware, however, the left-handed blackjack dealer. The way the spots are arranged on ordinary playing cards, it's a lot easier for him to take a quick peek.

2. Because the task has unexpected results when done left-handed. Many sports fall into this category. In tennis or Ping-Pong, for example, a righty opponent of a southpaw is faced with an unfamiliar spin and hop on the ball, and a ball that would be met by the weak backhand of a typical righty opponent becomes a strong lefty forehand. The same logic makes a left-handed boxer or fencer a person to be feared.

In biblical days, there was a tribe of Benjamin that had an army of left-handed soldiers. One heroic soldier named Ehud was able to slay the wicked King of Moab and lead the Israelites to safety. The palace guards who frisked him missed the dagger strapped to his right thigh, where they, being right-handed, would never think to look. Left on!

3. Because the task calls for skill and/or strength in both hands. Lefties climb trees, swim underwater, and mix batter better. They are also thought to make better piano players. In teaching the keyboard, the treble staff is taught first, then the bass is taught in relation to it. A lefty plays the bass more strongly and more easily, making for a more balanced performance.

4. Because the task calls for a different mental approach. Because lefties generally do more sharing of functions between the two hemispheres, they have a much higher recovery rate from strokes and other forms of brain damage. If, for example, the speech center of the dominant hemisphere is damaged, they have a much better chance than a righty of having the other hemisphere take over that function and allowing speech to continue.

In most righties, the sequential logic of "if A, then B" dominates thinking, and the intuitive, holistic hemisphere is subordinate. It is much too early in our understanding of the subject to do more than speculate, but evidence is starting to come in that lefties can solve certain kinds of problems much better (and others much worse) than righties. The day may come when the company president buzzes his secretary and says, "We are being done in by all those number-crunching planning types. What we need are some creative new strategies. Send in a lefty!"

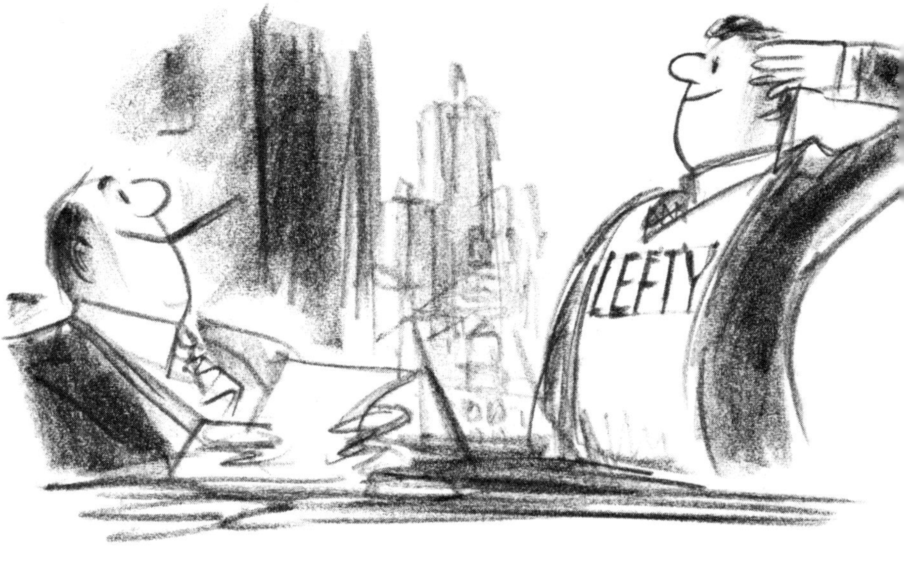
LEFTY

IS MOTHER NATURE LEFT-HANDED?

No. She's not right-handed either. Most inanimate objects and mechanical processes in the universe are symmetrical. If they have a spin or twist, they can perform it equally well in either the clockwise (right) or the counterclockwise (left) direction. There are some interesting exceptions, however.

Some natural forces have a preferred twist. Amino acids, a basic building block in living tissue, can be synthesized in the laboratory with either a right- or a left-hand twist. However, when they occur naturally, they always have a left-hand twist. The spin of the earth sets up a "Coriolis force," which determines the direction water takes swirling down a bathtub drain, or which way hair curls, depending on which hemisphere of the globe you're in.

Most living things are also physically symmetrical and move equally well one way or the other. A fish, for example, looks the same on its left side as on its right and swims both ways with the same facility. But here again there are some exceptions: Most climbing vines twine with a right twist. Honeysuckle (our favorite, naturally) twines to the left. The fiddler crab always has a left cutting claw; the narwhal has only a left tusk. Horses and elephants often show a preference for their left foot, and cats often prefer their left paw for touching and washing.

Humans are the biggest exception to Mother Nature. Not only do we have a nonsymmetrical appearance, but we have a differentiated brain and are predominantly right-handed. For theories on why, see the next chapter.

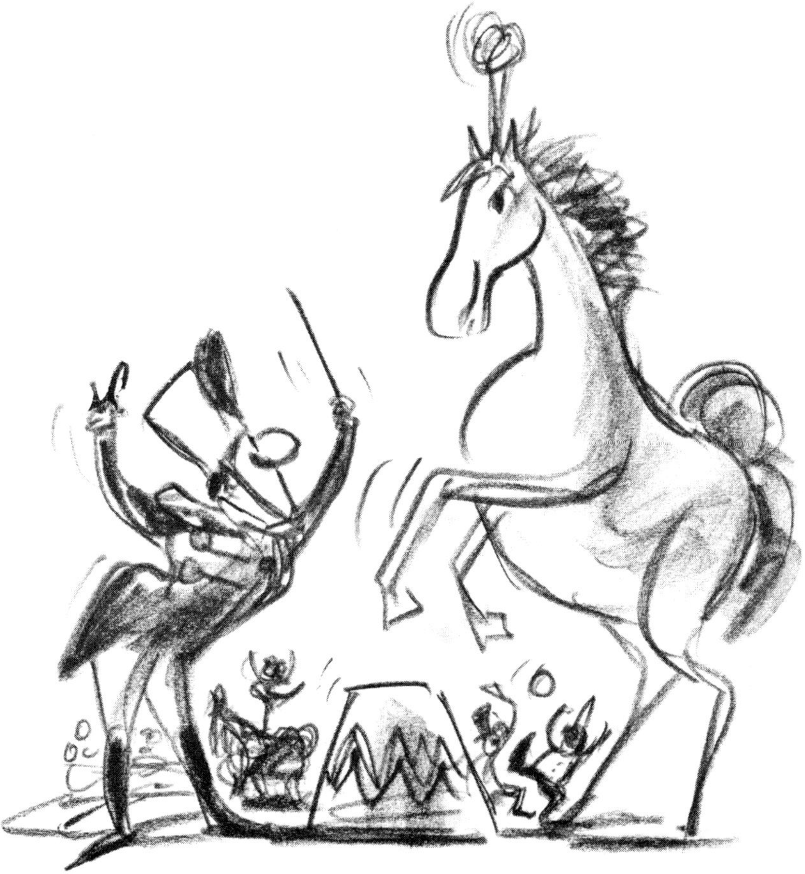

THE
GREAT
LEFTY
PUT-DOWN

"And before him shall be gathered all nations; and he shall separate one from the other, as the shepherd divideth his sheep from the goats. And he shall set the sheep on his right hand, but the goats on the left. Then shall the King say unto them on his right hand, 'Come, ye blessed of my Father, inherit the kingdom prepared for you from the foundation of the world. . . .' Then shall he say unto them on the left hand, 'Depart from me, ye cursed into everlasting fire, prepared for the devil and his angels. . . .' "

So said St. Matthew. Similar pleasantries about lefties can be found in the Old Testament, and the writings of Buddhism, Hinduism, Islam, Shinto, and the Aztecs, among others.

The great lefty put-down is deeply rooted in language; not just English, but all languages, ancient and modern. In Latin the word for left-handed is *sinister* (evil), in French it's *gauche* (awkward), in Italian it's *uncino* (crooked), and in Spanish it's *zurdo* (clumsy).

Language gives lefties a double whammy. Not only do we refer to a "left-handed compliment" or say someone is "out in left field," but a lefty must use "right" references to express good thoughts, such as "a right-hand man," "a dextrous person," the "right answer," and "getting off on the right foot."

A shining exception to all this is the language of classical Greece, where the word for left is *aristera*, which means superior, fine, the best. It is the root for the word *aristocrat* (and now you know how, in all modesty, we came to choose our company name).

Lefties are also thought to have a higher percentage of stutterers, poor readers, epileptics, and even schizophrenics. This may be true, but the statistics that "prove" it need careful scrutiny.

Lefties are also handicapped by the tools they are forced to use, the environment they are forced to live and work in, and the biases of those who teach them (we'll go into more detail later).

Well, there's no doubt that simply being a lefty is quite a challenge. The interesting questions are why, and what can be done about it?

Most of the civilized world is, and as far as we can tell, has always been right-handed. Evidence in the form of tool design and the use of weapons has been found as far back as the Bronze Age (curiously enough, the evidence of artifacts found from the Stone Age is far less conclusive) and explanations range from suckling habits to divine

21

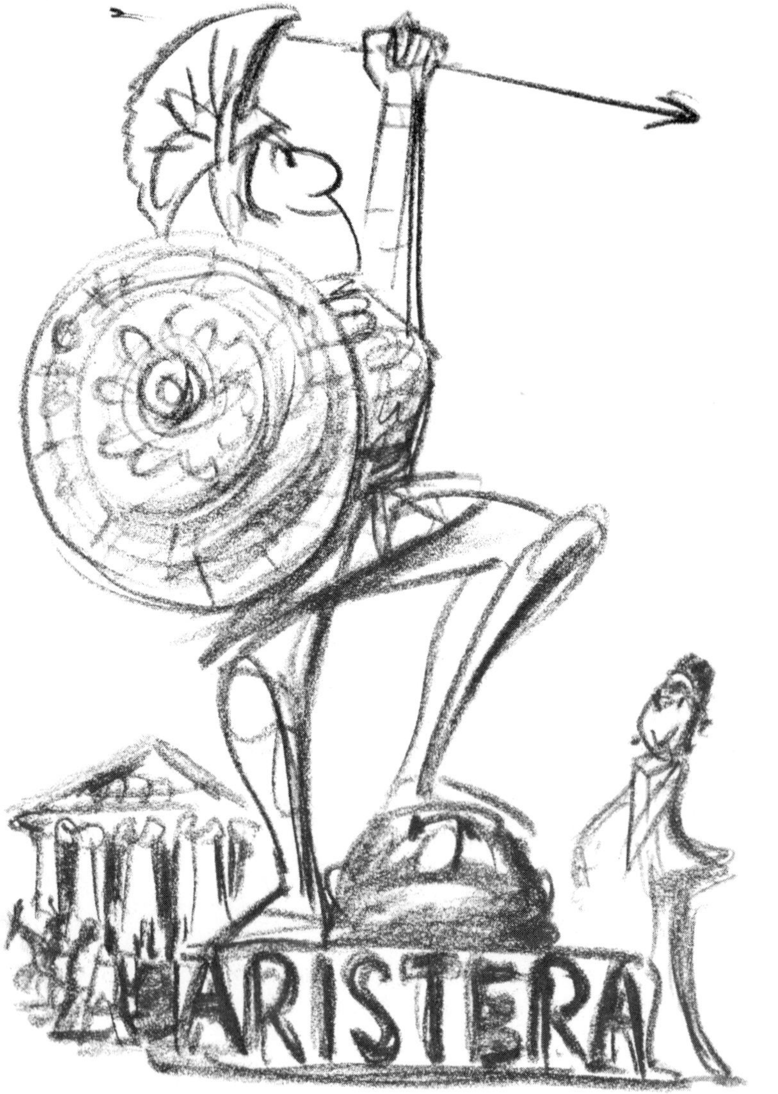
ARISTERA

law. To us, the most exciting explanation of why humans are predominantly right-handed can be found in Julian Jaynes's book, *The Origin of Consciousness in the Breakdown of the Bicameral Mind,* which relates handedness to the dawn of consciousness in the human mind.

Let's just take it as a fact that civilization is and always has been right-handed, and on that basis explore why that has brought about the Great Lefty Put-down. Here too, theories abound; which one(s) do we choose? The brilliant animal behaviorist, elder scientist, and Nobel Laureate Konrad Lorenz was once asked how he stayed so young. "Every morning," he replied, "I throw out a pet theory before breakfast."

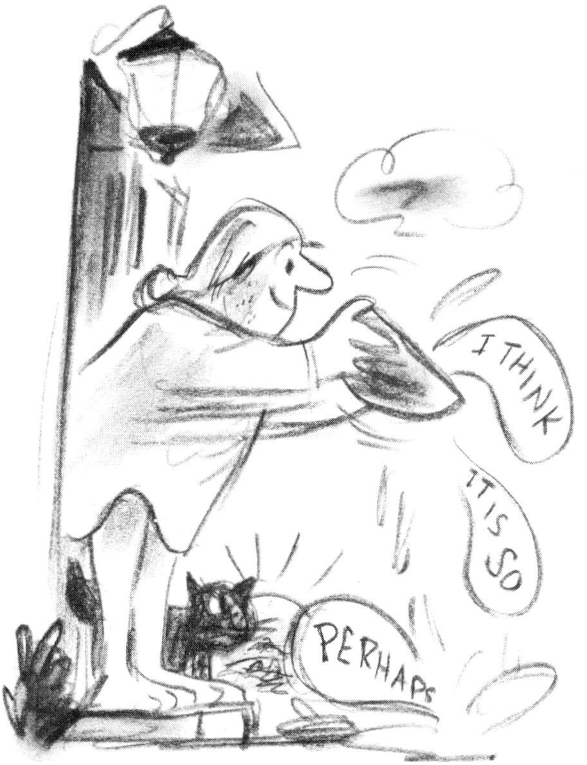
I THINK
IT IS SO
PERHAPS

After following that good advice we are left with two theories that make enough good sense to hang on to and pass along. They are:

1. The Theory of the Missing Toilet Paper

We are indebted to Dr. Carl Sagan for this theory. In his book, *The Dragons of Eden*, Dr. Sagan argues that toilet paper is a late invention. For most of human history, a hand alone (sometimes helped along by leaves) had to do the job. This chore was taken by the left hand, which became "unclean," and the right hand was used for making contact with people and for eating. This tradition is still very much alive in the Moslem countries. People who preferred to eat or touch their fellows with their left hand were aesthetic and hygienic menaces and were to be avoided.

2. The Theory of Righties' View of Their Own Left Hand

This is a speculative by-product of what we now know about the organization and functions of the human brain. Right-handed persons traditionally view their left side with contempt. ("Not so!" the sophisticated righty might object. But alas, it has been so.) Their left hand is weaker, less easily controlled, less willing to do what it is commanded. It is ruled by the right brain, which is the dreamy, dark side of the personality. With a completely illogical but human inference, righties associate their feelings about their own left hand to left-handed people.

In a future edition of *The Lefty's Survival Manual* we may have thrown these two theories out before breakfast, but for the moment they're the best that we have.

The question of what can be done about it remains. We have some very specific advice to parents, teachers, corporations, and anyone else who's interested in later chapters. But first, let's tell you exactly what's wrong.

LEFTY GRIPES
AND
GRIEVANCES

We decided to turn the tables on professors Dexter and Sinister. We gave *them* a quiz, and asked them to tell us how they saw the problems and frustrations facing a lefty in a right-handed world.

Professor Sinister didn't bother with details but started to look for an overall pattern. He said: "Some gripes deal with using tools and equipment meant for right-handed people on a day-to-day basis. Some of these examples, such as scissors, are obvious, but others hurt lefties in very subtle ways. Other grievances deal with the general environment a lefty has to deal with. Again, some of these situations, such as going through a turnstile, are obvious, but some, like using a pencil sharpener, are more subtle."

With perfectly sound right-handed logic, professor Dexter started to compile a detailed list. As you'd expect from a healthy right-hander suffering from myopia about lefty's problems, the list was a bit skimpy, so we enlarged it with information from our own files. Blending Sinister's pattern with Dexter's lists, we came up with this:

Products/obvious

Scissors

Vegetable peelers

Mitts

Slot machines

Instruction manuals for crochet, needlepoint, etc.

Wallets

Can openers

Golf clubs

Cabinet and refrigerator doors

Checkbook stubs

Ladles with lips on the right side

Key cases

Products/subtle

Car dashboard design/ ignition switch placement

Wind-up toys

Salad and cake forks (cutting tines)

Pinball machines

Serrated knives

Fly-front underwear

Shirt pockets

Ties with inside thickening cloth cut wrong

Gum wrappers

Twist ties for bags

Calculators/zero and total keys

Pens that smudge

Jewelry clasps

Playing cards

Zippers

Thermometers

Measuring cups

Wedding ring on working hand

Tennis racket handle winding

Injector razors

Spiral-bound notebooks

Thumbnail groove on pocket knives

Environment/obvious

Telephone booth design/closing doors, inserting coins, dialing

Writing arms on school chairs

Certain group activities, e.g., playing violin in an orchestra, where a lefty would poke their righty companion in the face with their bow

Certain sports/polo, hockey

Turnstiles

Environment/subtle

Office lighting

Golf courses

Attitudes of teachers, coaches, testers

Doorknobs

Voting machines

Pencil sharpeners

Place settings at meals

Cup handles

Faucets

Idioms and expressions

Did we leave any out? Let us know!

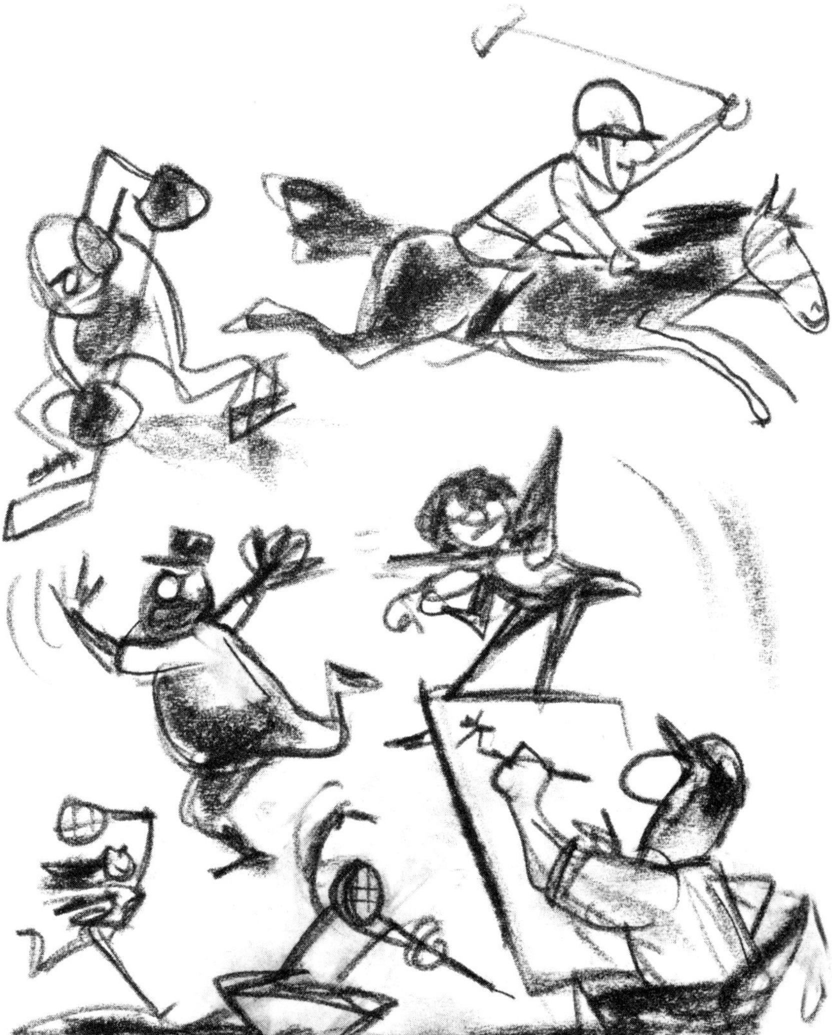

LEFTY AWARENESS AND CONDITIONING

Our friend Professor Dexter from the psychology department fancied himself something of a humorist. His students did not always agree. The professor was an ardent behaviorist, devoting many lectures to the subject of conditioning. His students believed in the effectiveness of conditioning but found Dexter's lectures and examples of drooling dogs and pecking pigeons boring. They discussed this one day with their faculty advisor, Creative Arts Professor Sinister, who whispered a plot in their ears.

The next morning, Professor Dexter happened to tell his first bad joke while standing in the right half of the hall, near the door. The class chuckled. The next two jokes, told while he was standing in the left half of the hall, were met with silence. A joke told when he was back on the right-hand side, partway to the door, was greeted with appreciative laughter. As the morning wore on, jokes on the left brought silence, those on the right brought laughter. Professor Dexter found himself spending more and more time in the right half of the hall. By the time the closing bell rang, he was almost out the door! It was the most enjoyable lesson in conditioning the class ever had.

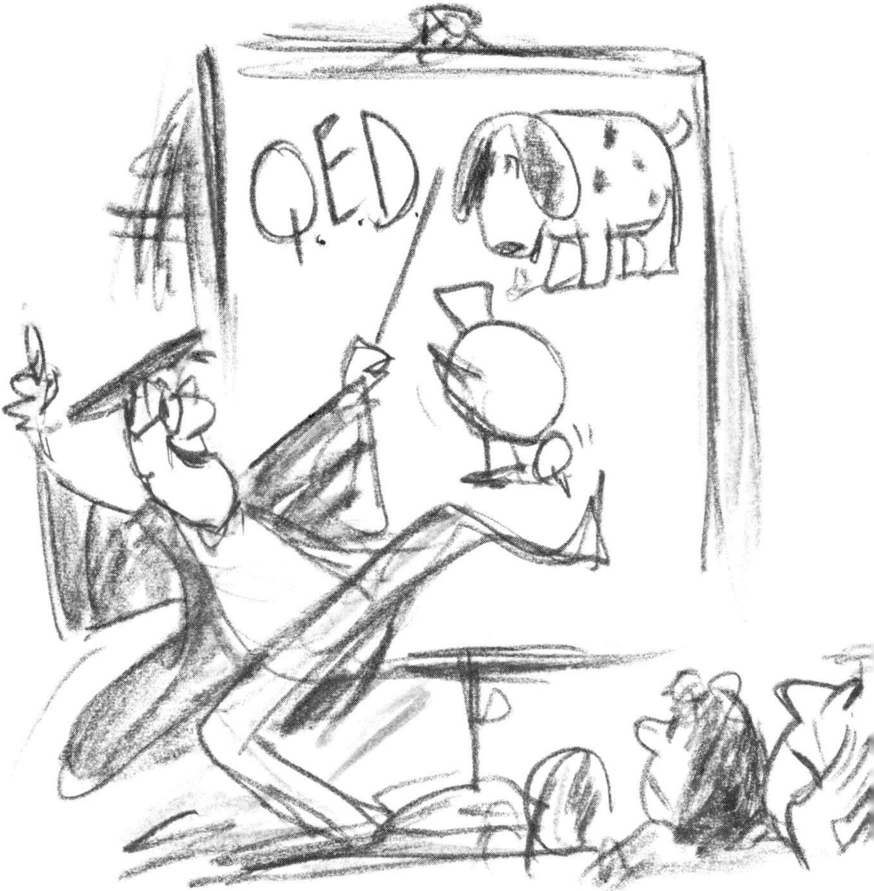
Q.E.D.

So what does this all have to do with lefties? The evidence is strong that left-handedness is primarily an inherited (and recessive) trait, but that's not to say that lefties don't acquire many of their physical and personality traits through conditioning. The tendency of lefties to be bilateral, that is, to have skills in both hands, may have a genetic basis but is certainly reinforced by the conditioning of a hostile environment. The fact that lefties often test out higher than righties on "oppositeness" indexes, which measure rebelliousness and lack of social conformity, may well be a reaction to all the conflicts they encounter in living in a right-handed world.

A curious example of the blend of inherent brain structure and conditioning lies in a study of faces. Hold a mirror to your face, with the edge at the middle, splitting your nose. You will see two left sides or two right sides and you won't recognize either! We all have a left face and a right face, which are never exact mirror images of each other. You know your mirrored face; everybody else knows your real face. For most of us who complain that a photo is "just not me," all it takes is looking at the photo in a mirror to see the "real you."

Julian Jaynes' book has a fascinating diagram of two faces, one an exact mirror image of the other. Study them for a minute.

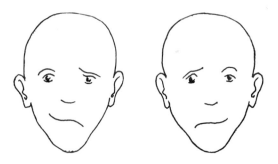

Decide which is more appealing. For most righties, the face on the left, with the left half smile, will look better. The left side of an object gets processed first by the right hemisphere, which is better adapted to dealing with images. (The right hemisphere also processes the right half image, but that information arrives a little later, since it goes through the left hemisphere first.) A team of researchers from Columbia and the University of Pennsylvania have suggested that people quickly sense that one-half of their face is seen as more attractive and better received emotionally, and they tend to condition their expression accordingly, making the left half their public face more bland or more cheerful and saving their emotional expression for the right half. We can speculate that for many lefties the "natural" situation is reversed, giving them an extra problem in social conditioning and in "putting on a happy face."

As we've mentioned before, another source of irritation lefties have had to cope with, is the use of tools and equipment righties take for granted. Consider the following:

- Ordinary scissors have blades that hide the cutting edge when used left-handed. Besides, they hurt!
- Instruction manuals are written for righties. Try to tie your shoes while you're looking in a mirror, and you'll get a feeling for the problems.
- Ladles and saucepans have the lip on the outside when used left-handed, perfect for spilling sauce in your lap.
- Corkscrews turn in your weakest direction. So do can openers and jar lid openers.
- Serrated knives cut sloppily.
- Spiral-bound notebooks hurt when your arm rests on the binding. It also interferes with your writing.

- Pens smear when you drag your hand across the word you just wrote.
- Rulers draw lines with pits and squiggles when you push instead of pull.

Many lefties have conditioned themselves to adapt to these fiendish devices, but many also go through life feeling a little bit awkward, a little bit clumsy. Society has conditioned them to believe that it "comes with." Don't you believe it! When a lefty is fitted out with properly designed tools, equipment, and instruction manuals, life can be beautiful (and comfortable) indeed.

We have titled this chapter "Lefty Awareness and Conditioning." Why the "awareness"? Because being aware helps by itself: being aware that society, if left to its own devices, can do to lefties what was done to unsuspecting Professor Dexter, and push them right out the door; being aware that lefties are really something very, very special and should be free to blossom in their own special way.

ADVICE TO PARENTS AND TEACHERS

Attention all right-handed parents and teachers! Try this:

- Put your wristwatch on your right wrist. Set and wind it.
- Open a locked door with the key in your left hand.
- Sharpen a pencil, using your left hand to turn the crank.
- Screw a screw into a board with your left hand.
- Dial a telephone number with your left hand.
- Cut a piece of soft cloth with a scissors in your left hand.
- Write your name left-handed.

How did you feel while doing these things? Were you comfortable? Sure, you *did* them all right, but it certainly wouldn't be your first choice the next time. Now imagine you're a child, and some adult is insisting that the way you just did these things was the proper way. Imagine that adult scolding and correcting you every time you tried to do these things the more natural, comfortable way—

right-handed—for you. How would you feel—bewildered? frustrated? unjustly treated? all of these at once?

Now picture what goes on in the mind of a lefty child when the situation is reversed. Remember that for most of you there weren't any of these things that you couldn't do if an adult *insisted* on it. It's simply that doing it their way made you feel uncomfortable and clumsy (and sometimes downright unhappy), and there was no way you could explain or give a good reason *why*.

To be fair, these adults need some understanding too.

They're not mean or uncaring. They are, on occasion, just unthinking. They've been conditioned by society to view right-handed ways as natural and correct. In trying to force the lefty child to conform to the "norm," the parent, teacher, coach, or troop leader could unwittingly cause the lefty a lot of grief—unless they've read this chapter.

"OK! OK!" you say. "Let me up. I get the point. But suppose we're talking about an infant or a toddler. Can't I train them one way or the other?"

Fair question! Up to the age of two or three, most chil-

dren tend to use both hands interchangeably. Some will be "naturally" lefty or righty, others can be trained. The years to watch carefully are when the child is between three and six, when the nervous system has matured enough for handedness to emerge.

We've formulated some simple guidelines, based on our research, experience, and philosophy.

1. *Everybody should develop a dominant hand.* It's more important that one hand dominate the other than it is which hand dominates. The same is true for eyes and feet. It's nice if they all have the same dominance, but it's not that serious if dominance is mixed. The most important thing is that the child knows clearly which hand and foot is dominant and feels comfortable about it. Children who are confused over which hand or foot to use can develop emotional as well as physical problems that will affect their performance in all areas of their lives.

2. *Look for signs of preference and reinforce them to establish dominance.* Notice which hand the child uses to reach for a toy or tool; to eat with; to draw with; to lift with. Once you have noticed a clear preference, reinforce it by handing or placing objects in the preferred hand, and by praise.

3. *Beware of your own subconscious bias.* Don't automatically place a spoon or toy in the child's right hand. Don't ever scold or "correct" the child if he wants to do it "the other way." The dangers of forcing right-handedness are probably not as catastrophic as they were once thought to be, but it's just not a sound idea for health and happiness.

This advice is fine for children who show a preference for one hand over the other. But suppose your child doesn't?

4. *If your child shows no preference, nudge him toward the right.* Remember, it's important to give your child the blessings of a dominant hand. We're just being practical when we recommend a nudge to the right; if you prefer the left, we'd be the last to object! Either way, do it by putting the spoon or toy in the hand you want to dominate. But nudge, *don't judge!* Your child may just be a little late in developing its own mind on the subject. Watch for a preference for the left that might show up later.

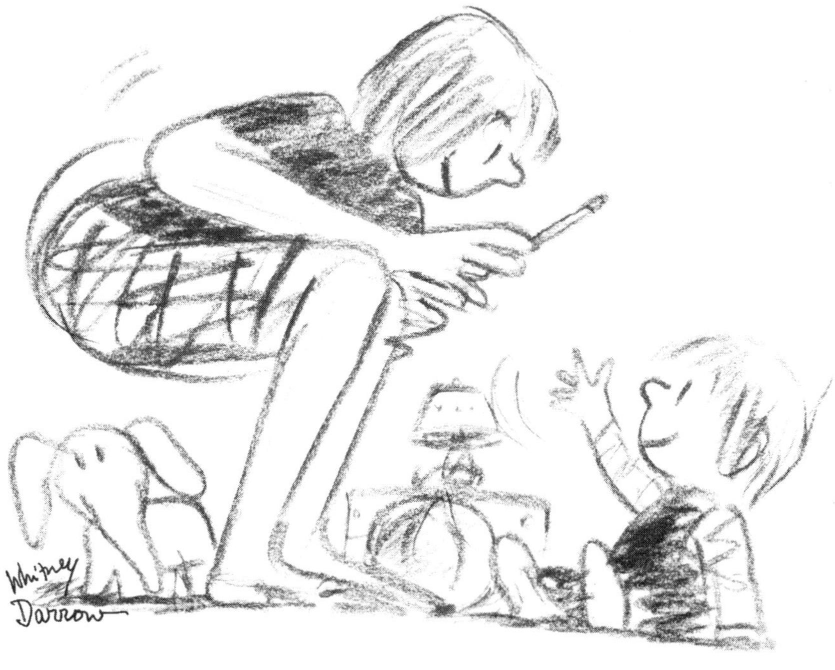
Whitney
Darrow

A customer of ours, a lovely and brave lady, told us that her twenty-three-year-old son had had to have his right arm removed at the shoulder. For a week before he came home from the hospital, she and every other member of the family lived with their right arms tied behind their backs. By the time her son came home, they had an idea of what he was going to be up against.

We are seldom called on to take such drastic action or rise to such heights, but the principle is the same. Don't assume that what is easy for you is easy for your child, or that your way is the only way. Look with love on the things that make us different.

When your child is tested:

The world is overflowing with test-happy scientists and test-groggy children. Lefty children are particularly good targets. Much of this testing is useful and good. Indeed, there are helpful tests you can give your child that can be found in some of the books listed in the catalog.

However—there are dangers. The test may have a built-in bias, and test results are easily misinterpreted. Let's call in our two learned friends to demonstrate.

Professor Dexter was very excited; he had just proved that grasshoppers hear through their legs. He had set up the experiment like this: A grasshopper was placed on a laboratory table. The professor struck a tuning fork; the grasshopper jumped. Then Professor Dexter wrapped up the grasshopper's front legs. He placed it on the table and again struck the tuning fork. This time, the grasshopper did not jump. The good professor concluded that grasshoppers hear through their legs.

"That's silly!" you may object, "the professor got his cause and effect all jumbled up." Of course he did, but so have a lot of other people. Let's look at an earlier experiment the professor designed. It was supposed to test a theory that one could tell a lefty from a righty by spreading the fingers of each hand to form a *V* with two fingers on

40

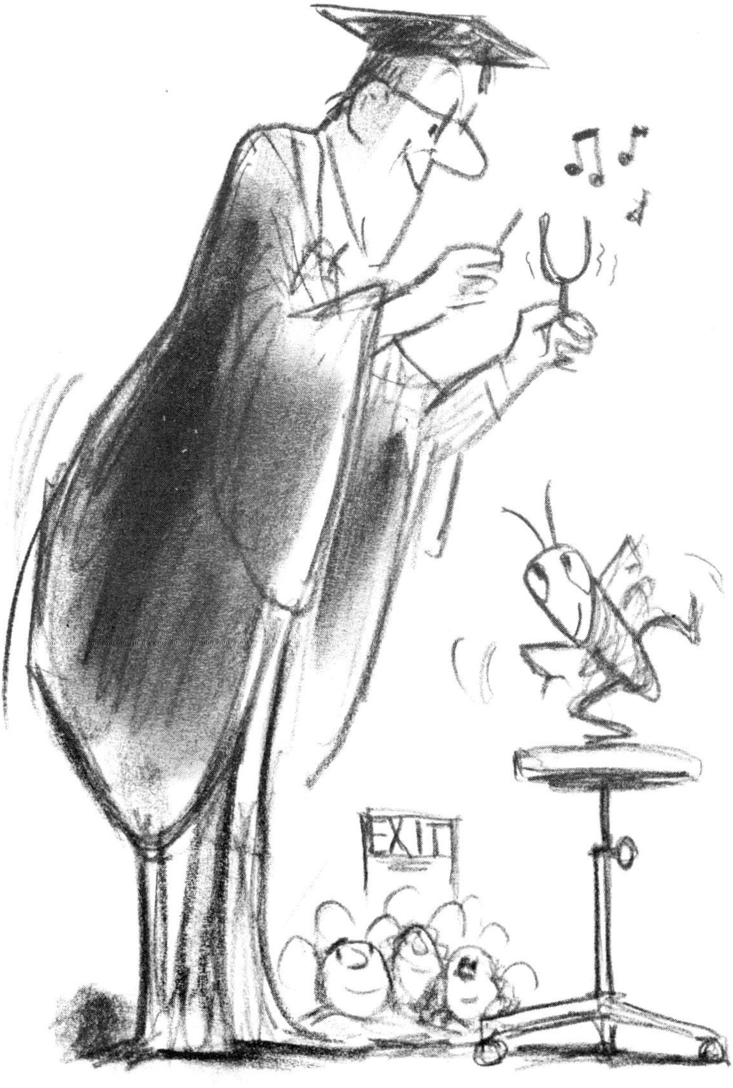
EXIT

each side; the hand with the bigger spread was the sub-dominant hand. Professor Dexter tested a hundred students and announced that the results confirmed the theory "with 90 percent accuracy." But wait a minute. We know that lefties make up about 10 percent of the population, so all that the professor had to do was guess "right-handed" every time and he would achieve 90 percent accuracy.*

Sometimes test results aren't valid because the test contains an unconscious bias on the part of the test designer. For years Professor Dexter claimed that righties were quicker than lefties in comparing numbers, using as evidence the results of a test set up like this:

A	B	C
142	017	
386	368	
204	402	
204	224	

and so on.

The test was a race against time. The students had to compare the numbers in columns A and B. If A was greater than B they put an X in column C; if A was less than B they put a check in column C. Year after year, the right-handed students finished more quickly than the left-handed students, proving the professor's theory.

When Professor Sinister joined the faculty, he heard about Dexter's experiment and asked to see the test itself.

*By the way, this test may be valid. It's just wise to be cautious about interpreting statistics.

One quick look and out came paper and pencil; Professor Sinister redesigned the test to look like this:

A	B	C
142		017
386		368
204		402

and so on.

With an indulgent shrug, Professor Dexter agreed to use the revised test on his next batch of students. Lo and behold, this time lefties and righties tested to be equally adept. What the good professor had been "proving" all those years was that if you force a lefty's hand to move further on a piece of paper, he'll take longer to write something down. Of course, it's also interesting to note that Professor Sinister perceived the catch in the test so quickly.

What is the point we're trying to make in this section? That all testing is nonsense and all statistics are untrustworthy? Not at all. Experiments and tests are vital to gaining insight into the nature of handedness. Besides, it's fun. But whenever we are tempted to toss in another fact or figure to fascinate ourselves and you, it's prudent to have the professors Sinister and Dexter around to remind us that statistics are not always what they seem and that tests can be designed (albeit innocently!) to prove what the designer wanted to prove. So enjoy along with us, but be careful!

A Special Note on Handwriting

Handwriting is often a special cause of misery for the lefty child, deserving special emphasis and attention.

1. *Make sure your lefty is comfortable.* This means good posture, a correct grip on the writing instrument, and correct positioning of the paper. There are several books and manuals that will give you detailed information. Specially designed notebooks that open "the other way" will avoid pinched arms and the contortions that go with trying to avoid the obstruction. You'll find the books, manuals and notebooks in the catalog section.

2. *Neatness counts.* Lefties tend to drag the side of their hand (and arm) over the word they just wrote, causing smudging. Pencils with hard lead and pens with fine points and quick-drying ink are invaluable to the lefty child (and adult). These are also listed in the catalog.

You'd be amazed at how big a difference good writing habits and tools can make. Attitude toward school can improve, and marks often go up.

WHAT CORPORATIONS AND GOVERNMENT CAN DO

Our two learned friends got up to leave. "Hold on a minute," we said, "you're not through yet. Now that you've come up with the gripes, tell us what corporations and governments can do about them." With that, we turned on the tape recorder and left the room. When we returned, Dexter and Sinister were gone. A transcription of their conversation follows.

D: He's a real pest. Now we're going to be late for our golf game.

S: I know. He does have a point, though. If we're going to raise corporate and government consciousness about the problems lefties face, positive action is needed. They're not going to discover the lefty market overnight, and we're going to need everything from appliances to underwear. We've got to get designers to consider the "handedness" of products early in the design process.

D: How do we motivate them to do that? Won't it cost more?

S: Not if the product is conceived and designed with handedness in mind. Besides, it will give the manufacturers a competitive edge.

D: So how do we get them to see the light?

S: By using the influence and power of groups such as school districts, municipalities, military supply units, and large corporations.

D: I see! In addition to requiring specific standards of safety, and reliability, they can also require ease of use *for either hand*, for products and equipment that they use.

S: Exactly. If a purchase order included a requirement either that an item be inherently easy for lefties to use or that a lefty version of it be made available, you'd be surprised how many manufacturers would start to pay attention. Especially if it meant increased sales.

D: So how do we get this to happen?

S: One step at a time. It doesn't have to happen over-night. Many readers of *The Lefty's Survival Manual* sit on school boards or hold local government office. Others are involved with corporations that do mass purchasing. It'll be like the proverbial camel whose master allowed him to stick his nose inside the tent.

Pretty soon the camel was completely inside. If we start soon and small and then keep nudging, someday there could be lefty versions of everything.

D: I like the way you think! You've earned that golf date.

S: See you on the first tee.

End tape.

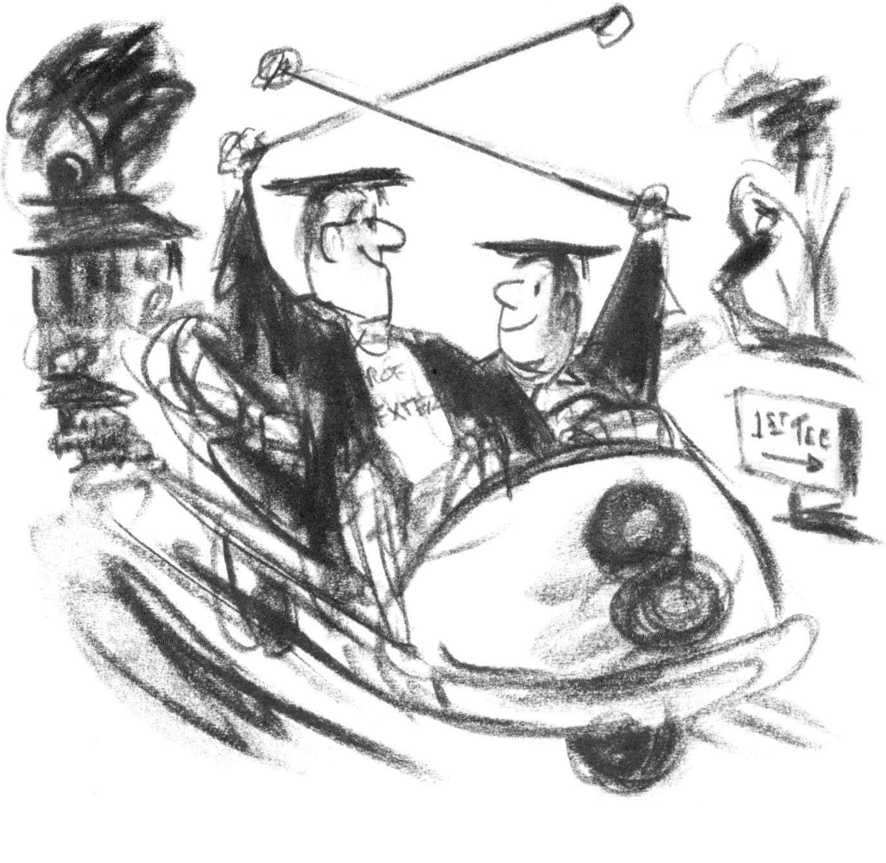
1ST TEE

WHAT DOES THE FUTURE HOLD?

For Lefties in particular:

Less irritation, more grace in daily life as lefty consciousness is raised and more and better tools and equipment become available.

For Everyone:

Richer, deeper, more meaningful life's work, as research on the relationship between handedness and the brain unfolds.

For a description of fine products designed with lefties in mind, and how to order them, turn now to the catalog section.

BIBLIOGRAPHY

Books

Barsley, Michael. *Lefthanded People*. No. Hollywood, Calif.: Wilshire Book Co., 1979. (A look at left-handedness in history, religion, art, language, and social customs.)

deKay, James T. *The Left-Handed Book*. New York: M. Evans & Co., 1966. (A humorous look at trials and tribulations of lefties.)

Delacato, Dr. Carl H. *A New Start for the Child with Reading Problems*. New York: David McKay & Co., 1977. (A provocative and unusual theory relating handedness and reading problems. Good material on handedness testing.)

Gardner, Martin. *The Ambidextrous Universe*. New York: Charles Scribner's Sons, 1979. (Recently updated and revised edition of the classic look at handedness in nature.)

Jaynes, Julian. *The Origin of Consciousness in the Breakdown of the Bicameral Mind*. Boston: Houghton Mifflin, 1977. (Don't let the jaw-breaking title throw you. This is a highly readable and startling theory on how man arrived at his modern mind. Sheds new light on religious and social history.)

Ornstein, Robert. *The Psychology of Consciousness*. New York: Viking Press, 1971. (An excellent explanation of right/left brain findings and their implications for understanding what thinking is all about.)

Sagan, Carl. *The Dragons of Eden*. New York: Random House, 1977. (A great living scientist and writer traces the evolution of intelligence, with interesting sidelights on handedness.)

Silverstein, Alvin, and Virginia B. Silverstein. The Left-Hander's World. Chicago: Follett Publishing, 1977. (A general treatment of the subject. Very good for children.)

Newspaper and Magazine Articles

Ashby, Lynn, "Right on, left." Column.

Bombeck, Erma, "First Hand Left-Hand Info." Column.

"Brain hemispheres seen as vital factor in way we learn." *Wall Street Journal*, March 30, 1979, p. 1.

Doktor and Bloom, "Selective Lateralization of Cognitive Style Related to Occupation as Determined by EEG Alpha Symmetry." *Psychophysiology*, 14 (1977): 4.

Fuerman, George, "Post Card—Left-Out." Column.

Herron, Jeannine, "Southpaws, How Different Are They?" *Psychology Today*, March 1976.

Kerr, Alix, "What's Right for the Left-handed Child?" *Family Circle*, February 1969.

Kulhary, Raymond, "Some 'Handy' Information." Arizona State University.

"The Left Handed Minority." *Spectrum Magazine*, SRI, September–October 1978.

Levy, Prof. Jerre. Correspondence with Aristera, The Left Hand People. University of Pennsylvania, June 1975.

Mintzberg, Henry, "Planning on the Left Side and Managing on the Right." *Harvard Business Review*, July –August 1976.

Ornstein, Robert, "The Split and Whole Brain." *Human Nature Magazine*, May 1978.

"People Are Really Two-Faced." *Time Magazine*, December 11, 1978, p. 126.

Pines, Maya, "We are left-brained or right-brained." *New York Times Magazine*, September 9, 1973, p. 32.

Seidenbaum, Art, "From Left to Wrong." Column.

Sherman et al. "Cerebral Laterality and Verbal Process." *Journal of Experimental Psychology*, 2 (1976): 720–727.

Various articles. *Lefty Magazine*. Published by Lefthanders International, 3601 S.W. 29th, Topeka, Kansas 66614.

Veeck, Bill, "What's left for the left-handed?" "Speaking Out" Column.

Ziedel, Evan, "The Elusive Right Hemisphere of the Brain." California Institute of Technology: *Engineering and Science Magazine*, September–October 1978.

CATALOG

Introduction

Hello . . . and welcome to the wonderful world of fine products designed for lefties. I'm Pete Neiman, president of Aristera, The Left Hand People. This is our ninth year of pleasing lefties (and those who love them) with excellent quality and design, fast service, and personal attention.

Historically, lefties have been forced to adjust to tools and products designed for the right-handed person. We at Aristera feel it is always better to fit the tool to the human than to fit the human to the tool. Aristera products do this, and can relieve a very large number of the irritations that surround the daily life of a lefty. All of our products are covered by this simple *ANY REASON GUARANTEE: YOU MAY RETURN ANY ITEM FOR ANY REASON AND RE-CEIVE FULL PURCHASE PRICE REFUND.* Try us and enjoy. Order now! Open up a new world of grace, strength, accuracy, and comfort with products from Aristera, The Left Hand People.

For ease of reading and selection, we have divided the catalog into sections: Fastening/Holding/Carrying, Pouring/Serving, Slicing/Peeling/Opening, Scissors/Shears, Instruction Manuals, Writing, Reading All About It, Sports, and Lefty Pride Products.

Prices in this catalog are guaranteed through December 1980.

GIFT CERTIFICATE

C02 LEFTY GIFT CERTIFICATE. A gift certificate from the Left Hand People makes an ideal gift. Minimum amount $15.00, which covers merchandise and applicable postage and handling. With a certificate of $30.00 or more, P&H is free. Just fill in to whom it is to be sent. We'll fill out the certificate and immediately send it to the person you designate, and all gift certificates include a **free** "Lefty Survival Manual" and Lefty Carry-All (see item #E30 for description). Any product in the Manual or in the "What's New" bulletin can be ordered with the gift certificate. $15.00 & up

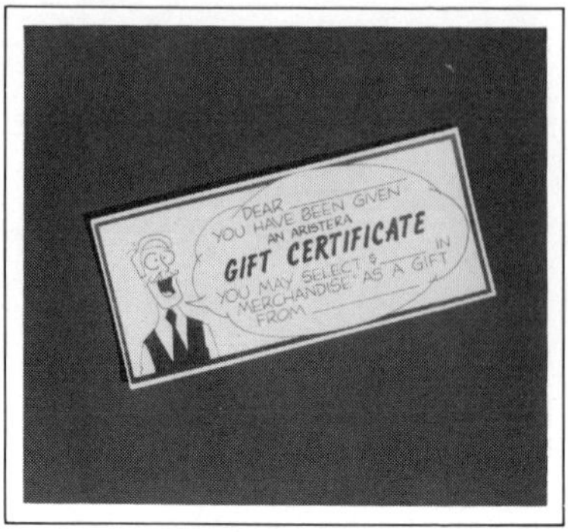
DEAR
YOU HAVE BEEN GIVEN
AN ARISTERA
GIFT CERTIFICATE
YOU MAY SELECT $ IN
MERCHANDISE AS A GIFT
FROM

FASTENING • HOLDING • CARRYING

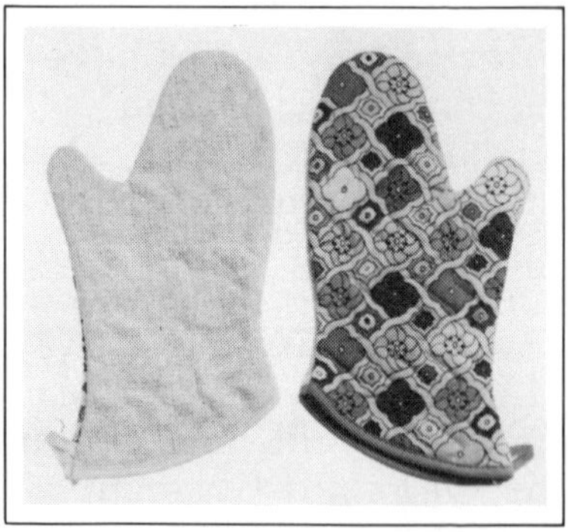

A40 LEFTY POTHOLDER MITT. Gaily quilted back, heat-resistant front. No need to buy a pair just to get a left hand! $2.25

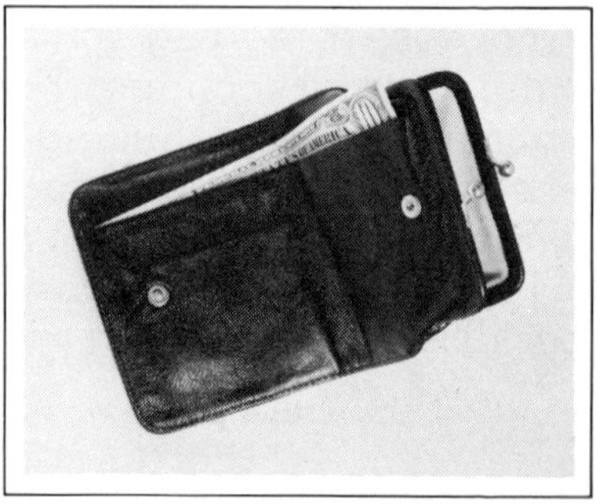

E20 LEFTY FRENCH PURSE. Genuine leather combination change purse and wallet. Designed so money goes in wallet the lefty way, and change doesn't fall out of purse. Choice of color: Tan, dark green, red, black. All with gold design. $9.95

E21   LEFTY KEY CASE.
Genuine leather. Snap front
opens the lefty way and holds 6
keys. Choice of color: Red,
black. $8.95

E11L   LEFTY BELT BUCKLE.
Fits on 1¾" belts the lefty way. No
more awkward contortions while
tightening your belt. Made from
genuine pewter. Select from
Whale, Horse, Sailboat, Lobster,
or Eagle design. $10.95

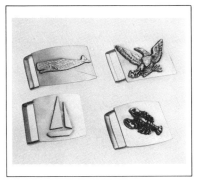

E11S   LEFTY BELT BUCKLE.
Same as E11L., but smaller to fit 1"
belt width. Available in Whale,
Horse, Sailboat, or Eagle design.
Ideal for women and children.
(Not Illustrated) $8.95

E30   LEFTY CARRY-ALL.
Approximately 12" x 16", very
lightweight, rugged, durable,
puncture-resistant polyethylene
tote bag. Has drawstring top for
easy closing and carrying. Handsome beige background with
word "Lefty" printed in many writing styles in rich dark brown. Has
many uses and is ideal for all
ages. $ .95
**AS A BONUS, with a purchase of
$15.00 or more, you receive a free
bag.**

E40   LEFTY WRISTWATCH
for men and boys. The winding
stem is beside the "9" position
(righty watches have the stem beside the "3" position). Much easier
to wind and set left-handed when
worn on right wrist. Swiss movement. Gift-boxed. Specify denim
or leather strap. $24.95

E41   LEFTY WRISTWATCH
for ladies and girls. Same fine
product as E40, but in elegant
feminine styling, with leather
strap. $29.95

J12   THIRD HAND TOOL.
Small objects can be held tightly
at any angle. Both hands then
free to solder, glue, paint, etc.
                            $10.95

K10   PLAYING CARDS.
Ordinary playing cards have the
numbers on only two corners.
Lefties will hide the numbers
when fanning cards in their natural way. They learn to hold them
in an uncomfortable manner.
These cards solve the problem by
putting the numbers on all four
corners. Simple, but what a bless-
ing! 2-deck set—Bring 'em with
you. $3.95

A20   LEFTY SOUP LADLE.
Has generous size pouring lip on
lefty and righty side. No more
mess! Two new features are a
color-coded top and a special lip
for hooking your ladle on the edge
of the pot so it won't slip in. $2.50

A50   LEFT-HANDED
MOUSTACHE MUG.
Sturdy,   handsome,   large-
capacity mug with moustache
guard on lefty side. Made of lead-
free stoneware. $11.95

A52   LEFTY MINIATURE
PITCHERS.
Elegant Ruby glass. 2 oz. pitchers
with lip on lefty side. Have many
uses. Different shapes make these
highly decorative. Order several,
and we mix shapes. $9.95

A55   LEFTY WARMER/SERVER.
Made from sturdy, lead-free,
oven-proof stoneware. Blue/
green color. Handle is set for left-
handed serving of gravy, melted
butter, sauces. $11.95

A56   **GRAVY LADLE.**
Has generous lips on lefty and righty sides. No more embarrassing spills. Exceptionally beautiful Georgian English design. Heavy silver plate. Complements any table decor. (Not Illustrated) $14.95

A57   **PUNCH LADLE.**
Same as A56, but in large punch bowl size. $24.95

A62A   **ICE CREAM SCOOP.**
The thumb lever to push out ice cream is in the middle, so either hand can use it. So sensible! $10.95

A62B   **ICE CREAM DIPPER.**
Designed to cut through the coldest ice cream because of a defrosting fluid sealed within. Comfortable-to-hold aluminum scoop without a thumb lever to wrestle with. Even little children can have fun easily scooping their own hard ice cream or ices. Easily cleaned, never wears out. $3.95

WOODEN KITCHEN TOOLS.
Each is shaped and edged for left-hand use. Working edges and corners are gentled for scratch-free performance on Teflon and delicate surfaces.

A63A   LEFTY SPATULA.
Made from strong, nonporous beechwood. Will not absorb cooking odors. $1.75

A63B   LEFTY MIXING SPOON.
Made from hard maple to take banging abuse. Special lefty corner to get into bowl crevices.
                                    $1.75

A63C   LEFTY SERVING FORK.
Made from soft, flexible birch for springiness. Use for both turning and serving. $1.75

A63D LEFTY TASTING SPOON.
Large bowl, beautifully shaped
channel for spill-free lefty tasting
of thick or thin foods. $2.75

A63S   Set of 4 tools per above.
                              $6.95 Save!

A64   MEASURING CUP/BEAKER.
Pint/cup/oz. measures are on lefty
side (metric measure on other
side) of "see-through" material.
Generous   pouring   lip.
Dishwasher-proof. Tall enough to
also serve as an attractive holder
for your wooden tools. $3.50

SLICING · PEELING · OPENING

A10   LEFTY CAN OPENER.
Comfortable grip with large,
easy-turning handle, operating
the lefty way. $8.95

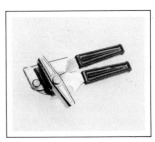

**A30A   AMBIDEXTROUS
                   PEELER/PARER.**
Lovely design, wooden handle
with stainless steel blade. Beautifully balanced tool for peeling in
either direction. $3.95

A30B   LEFTY PEELER/PARER.
Fine old English Import. For lefty
peeling **toward** body. $3.95

A31 GRATER/SHREDDER/SLICER.
Three separate drums can be set
into holder the lefty way. This is
the authentic, famous old Mouli
French tool. $7.50

A34   LEFTY BREAD KNIFE.
Serrated edge is ground for easy
left-hand cutting. Great for extra
thin slicing of any food. Finally, a
lefty can slice smoothly. $8.50

A37   COMBINATION KNIFE
AND FORK.
The side of the fork is specially
ground for lefty cutting. Cut food
and eat with just the left hand.
$24.95

A38 **LEFT-HANDED
BUTTER SERVER.**
This is an old-fashioned personal
butter server with a trowel-bent
handle and decorative blade. Extremely rare. Made from genuine
pewter. For left-hand use only.
Extra thoughtful gift idea. $9.95

A39 **LEFTY TOMATO KNIFE.**
Serrated edge is ground for lefty
use. Now a lefty can slice neatly
through soft fruits. Pointed tip
helps to take out potato eyes and
fruit bruises. Its utility size makes it
an excellent all-purpose lefty
knife. $4.95

A54 **LEFTY CHEESE SERVER.**
This rare, lovely piece is beautifully designed with a stainless
steel cheese blade set in a natural
stag horn handle. It is curved naturally for left-handed use. $9.95

A60   LEFTY CORKSCREW.
Specially designed for left-handed use with lefty spiral motion. Old-fashioned wooden handle. No more awkwardness when opening fine wines. $4.50

A61   LEFTY CORKSCREW, WING TYPE.
Same left action as A60, but more elegant. Greater pulling power from wing action. $12.95

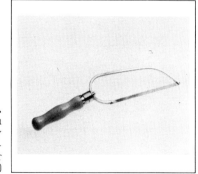

J10   HACKSAW.
Clever adjustable handle lets you saw with either hand, in any handle position. For hard-to-get-at items. Particularly useful for lefties. $7.50

J14A   LEFTY POCKETKNIFE.
The thumbnail groove is on the
lefty side, an important change
for lefty convenience. Single car-
bon steel blade folds into unbreakable handle. Precision Sheffield knife. $7.95

J14B   SINGLE-HANDED KNIFE.
Opens and closes easily with just
one hand. Unbreakable, non-slip
handle. Surgical steel blade.
                              $9.95.

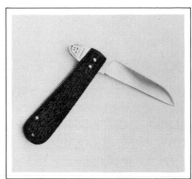

**J17   EASY OPENING DOOR
         KNOB ATTACHMENT.**
A handle attachment for round
door knobs. Eliminates awkward
knob twisting. A gentle touch on
the bar opens door. Attaches with
screwdriver in minutes. Great
also when hands are loaded with
packages. Fits almost all knobs.
                              $5.95

DXX LEFTY SCISSOR SERIES.
These are all finest quality in-
struments, with correct handles
and lefty blades. With top quality
lefty scissors such as these, lines
get cut straighter, without fingers
hurting.

**If you want a good all-around
scissor—order D23.**
**If you want a good all-around
scissor and you do a lot of fabric
cutting—order D06.**
**If you want a good all-around
scissor to safely carry with
you—order D24.**

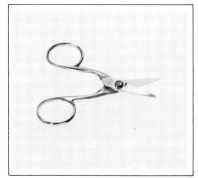

D01A   NAIL SCISSORS.
Straight Blades Precision Sheffield instrument. 3½" $8.95

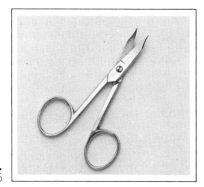

D01B   NAIL SCISSORS.
Curved blades. 3½" $11.95

D01C   CUTICLE SCISSORS.
Curved blades. 3½" $11.95

D02   CHILDREN'S BLUNT TIP.
Cushion-grip handles. 4" $1.35

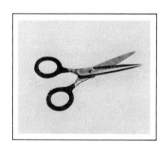

D03   CHILDREN'S POINTED TIP.
Cushion-grip handles. 5" $1.55

D04   6" SEWING SCISSORS.
$12.95

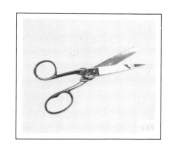

D05 Straight handle. 7" $15.95

D06 Bent handle, for fabric cutting and general use. 8" $17.95

D08   **PINKING SHEARS.**
Black handle. 7½" $15.95

D09   **BARBER SHEARS.**
7" $12.95

D12   **SHARP POINT
EMBROIDERY SCISSORS.**
Precision Sheffield scissors   3½".
(Not Illustrated. Similar to D01, except with thinner
blades.)   **$8.95**

D21   **GARDEN/KITCHEN
SHEARS.**
These are an ambidextrous,
"center anvil" design, but we love
them because they have a power-
ful ratchet design, which makes
pruning and bone cutting easy for
lefties.   **$12.95**

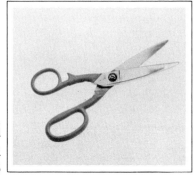

D22   **KITCHEN SHEARS.**
The classic design, but reversed
for lefties. Multipurpose handle,
precision Sheffield heavy-duty
blades.   **$19.95**

D23   **GENERAL USE.**
With plastic molded comfort-
shape handles. Very lightweight
and easy on fingers. Excellent for
cutting synthetics. 7½"   **$11.95**

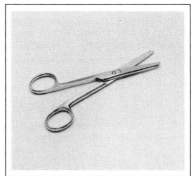

D24   NURSE'S SCISSORS.
Short blades with blunt tips. Use
for bandage scissors. Safe for
children to use, too. $14.95

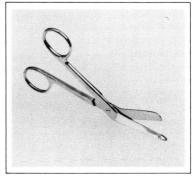

D25   LEFTY BANDAGE
SCISSORS.
With official bend in the blade
and flattened tips. $14.95

WRITING

B10A   LEFTY SPIRAL-BOUND
NOTEBOOK.
Opens left to right. No more cruel
arm pinching from leaning on spiral binding. Holes punched on the
outside. Perforated on the inside,
so pages end up neatly and correctly in 3-ring binder. 50 8½" x 11"
college ruled sheets. Lefty cover
decoration. Students love them.
$1.50

B10B LARGE LEFTY SPIRAL NOTEBOOK.
Same as B10A, except this size has 150 sheets and 3 subject divider pages. Excellent value.
(Not Illustrated) $2.95

LEFT HANDED
ADDRESS BOOK

B11 LEFTY ADDRESS BOOK.
Large cover. Pocket size. Alphabetized with easy *left thumb* indexing. Opens left to right. Gold-stamped lefty cover. Choice of red, black, green, blue. $4.95

J15A LEFTY RULER. 12″.
Numbers advance right to left. Made of hard aluminum. Professional precision marking. Will last many years. Helps lefties draw lines with confidence. $3.95

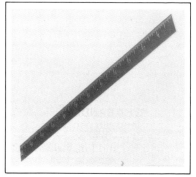

J15C LEFTY RULER.
12″/30cm. Old-fashioned wooden ruler with a modern touch—both metric and inch scales. Numbers advance from right to left. Helps lefties draw lines with confidence.
$1.25

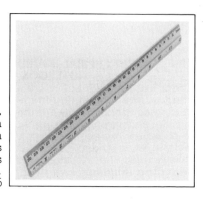

J20 ANIMATED "SMART" RULER. New metric/inch (17.5 cm/7") ruler. Lets lefties measure and draw lines the lefty way—numbers advance from right to left. With a flip of the wrist or a nod of the head, ruler changes to the righty way (doesn't discriminate against righties). Educational and fun way to inch your way into the metric system. A fantastic value. $ .95

Bonus option for orders over $15.00.

the lefty way
the lefty way

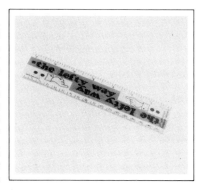

L10 LEFT-HANDED PEN SET. Classical fountain pen barrel plus 6 interchangeable points, for all sorts of plain and fancy penmanship. Comes with special lefty instructions for italics, etc. $7.50

Platignum Lettering Set
& Instruction Manual
Lettering
Lettering Set

L11 LEFTY PENCILS. Excellent quality with printed message: **THIS IS MY LEFTY PENCIL.** Reads correctly only when writing with left hand. Have some fun with your friends—now righties have to stand on their heads to read your pencils. 6/$1.00

Take advantage of our special offer. 24/$3.50

L12 LEFTY SOFT-TIP MARKER PEN.
Extra fine point and "immediate drying" ink keeps lefties from smudging through their own handwriting. Very popular! Printed with a cute poem, reads correctly only when writing with left hand. Set of 3 pens (blue, black, red). Set $2.25

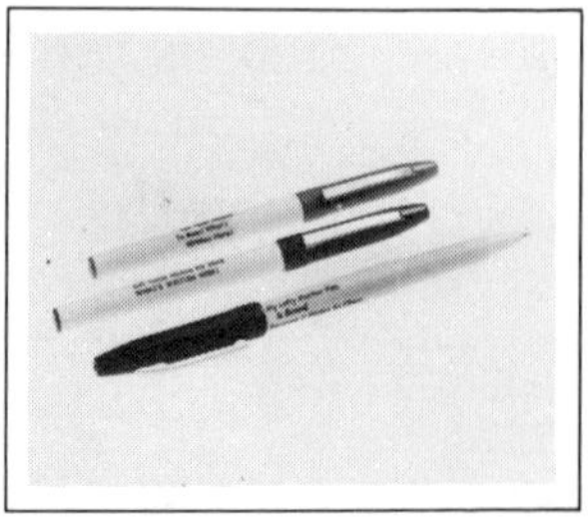

INSTRUCTION MANUALS

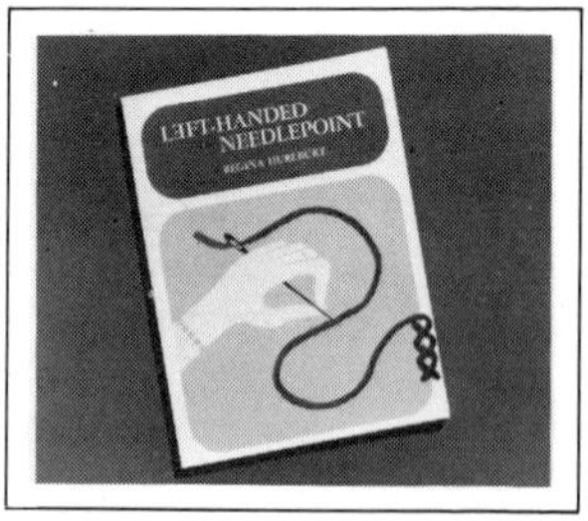
LEFT-HANDED NEEDLEPOINT

B21A LEFT-HANDED NEEDLEPOINT.
Good basic book. Explains plain and fancy stitches, designing your own needlepoint canvas, wool, and needles. Includes patterns and designs. Well illustrated. Exclusively for lefties. $4.50

B21B LEFT-HANDED KNITTING.
Same exciting features as B21A, but now devoted to knitting.
(Not Illustrated) $4.50

B21C LEFT-HANDED CROCHET.
3rd book in this fine series. Same appeal as earlier two; now devoted to crochet. (Not Illustrated) $4.50

B23C WRITING MANUAL FOR TEACHING THE LEFT-HANDED.
Classic text on left-handed writing. Covers body position, paper position, simple exercises, and much more. Produces attractive, neat lefty writing. $1.50

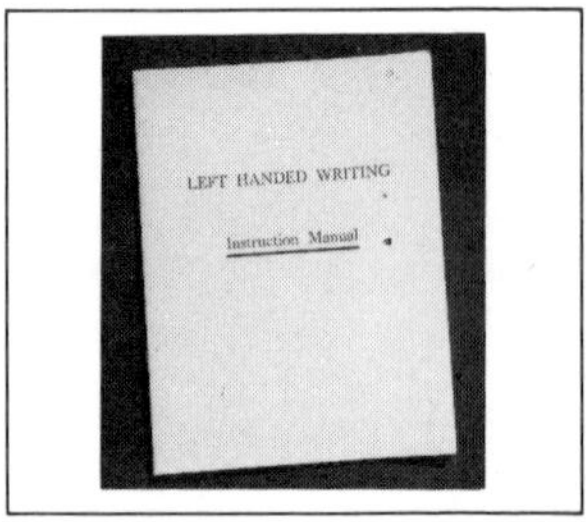
LEFT HANDED WRITING
Instruction Manual

B26 PRIMER OF LEFT-HANDED EMBROIDERY.
A very fine book for both beginner and advanced. For lefties exclusively. Beautifully and clearly illustrated with easy-to-follow directions for 55 stitches. $5.95

A
PRIMER OF
LEFT-HANDED
EMBROIDERY

B27 LEFT-HANDED GUITAR.
Instructions for left-handed guitar playing, plus "how to" section on restringing a righty guitar to make it left-handed. Includes nice old songs with lefty chords. $2.95

LEFT
HANDED
GUITAR

B29 This is the famous Step-by-Step series of color manuals, with both righty and lefty steps. They are good, inexpensive books.

B29A STEP-BY-STEP STITCHERY
$2.95

stitchery

STEP-BY-STEP
knitting

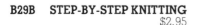

B29B STEP-BY-STEP KNITTING
$2.95

B29C **STEP-BY-STEP CROCHET.**
$2.95

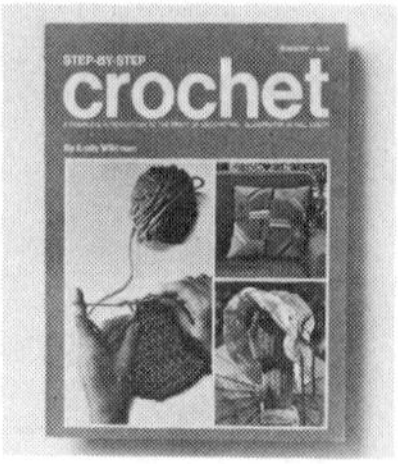
STEP-BY-STEP
crochet

READING ALL ABOUT IT

C01A **LEFTY'S SURVIVAL MANUAL.**
This is the Bantam edition of our book/catalog chockful of useful information on coping with lefty problems, product problems, and their solutions. Attractively illustrated with both photos and cute cartoons. Fun and informative. Excellent gift item. No postage and handling charges when ordered alone. $2.95

C01B **LEFTY SURVIVAL MANUAL.**
This is our basic catalog describing and illustrating products. It comes with bulletins showing recent additions to the product line. No postage and handling charges when ordered alone. $1.00

C10 THE LEFT-HANDED BOOK.
Humorous little book with cartoon illustrations of the trials and tribulations of lefties. Ideal for all ages.
$1.95

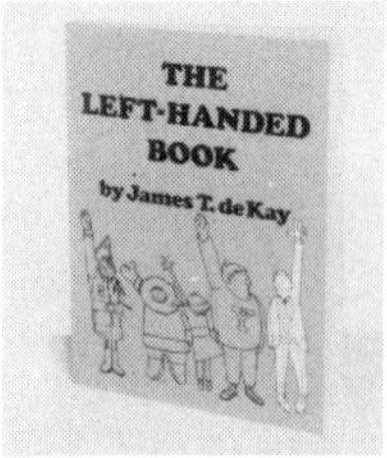
THE
LEFT-HANDED
BOOK
by James T. deKay

C11 LEFT-HANDED PEOPLE.
Fascinating look at left-handedness in history, religion, art, language, and social customs.
$2.95

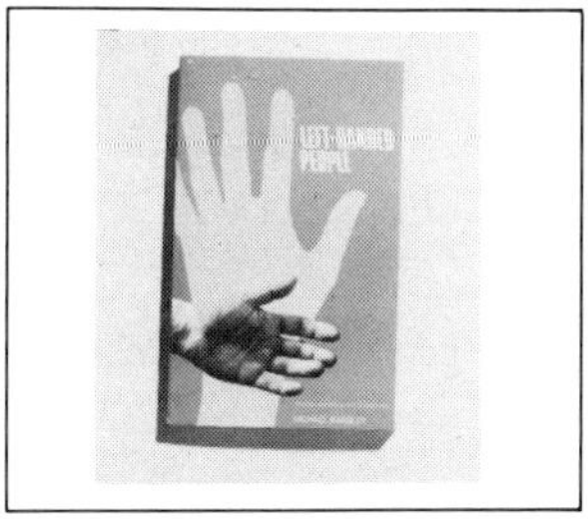
LEFT-HANDED PEOPLE

C12 AMBIDEXTROUS UNIVERSE.
For science-minded youngsters and adults. A look at left-handedness in the universe. Recently updated and revised to reflect the latest findings of physicists, biologists, and astronomers.
$9.95

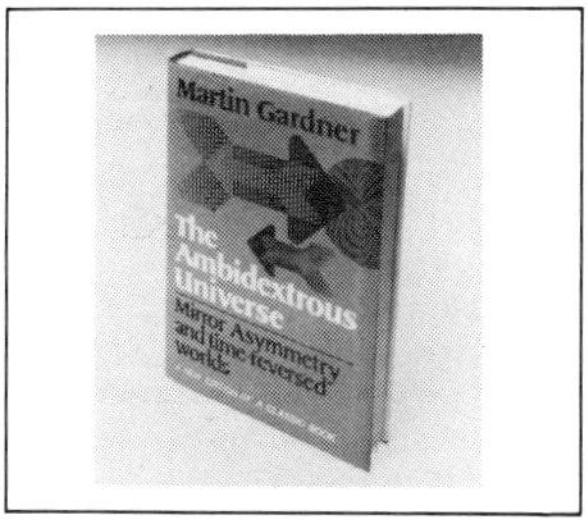
Martin Gardner
The Ambidextrous Universe
Mirror Asymmetry and time reversed worlds

C15 A NEW START FOR THE CHILD WITH READING PROBLEMS.
Interesting, provocative theory relating handedness and reading problems. $4.95

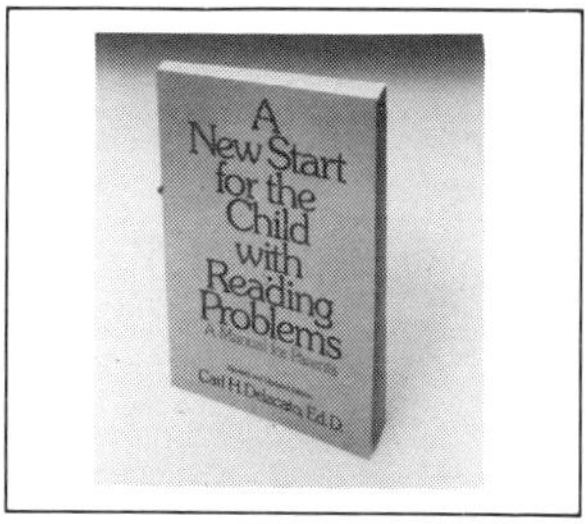
A New Start for the Child with Reading Problems
Carl H. Delacato, Ed.D.

C17 THE LEFT-HANDER'S WORLD.
An educational and informative book that answers questions like: Why are people left-handed? How are left-handers different from right-handers? and many more. Beautifully illustrated.
$5.95

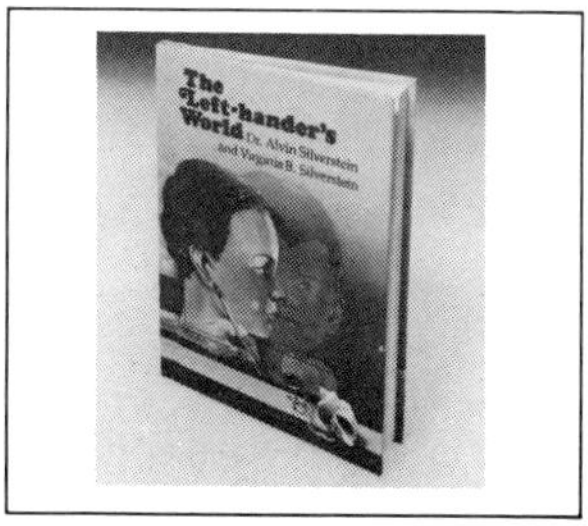
The Left-hander's World

C18 THE ORIGIN OF CONSCIOUSNESS IN THE BREAKDOWN OF THE BICAMERAL MIND.
Julian Jaynes. Don't let the jaw-breaking title throw you. This is a highly readable and startling theory on how man arrived at his modern brain. Sheds new light on religious and social history as well. $12.95

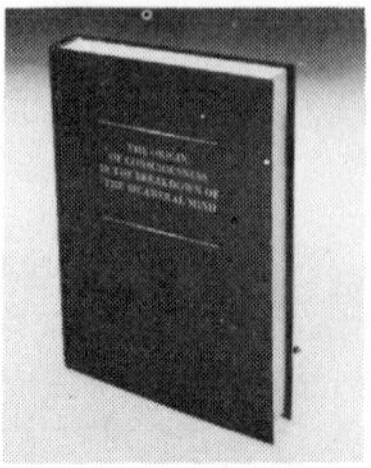

C19 THE PSYCHOLOGY OF CONSCIOUSNESS.
Robert Ornstein. Excellent explanation of right/left brain findings and their implications for understanding what thinking is all about. $8.95

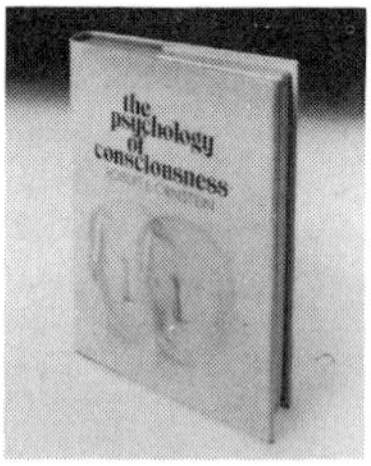
the psychology of consciousness

C20 THE DRAGONS OF EDEN.
Dr. Carl Sagan traces the evolution of intelligence, with interesting sidelights on handedness. Highly recommended for adults and youngsters. $8.95

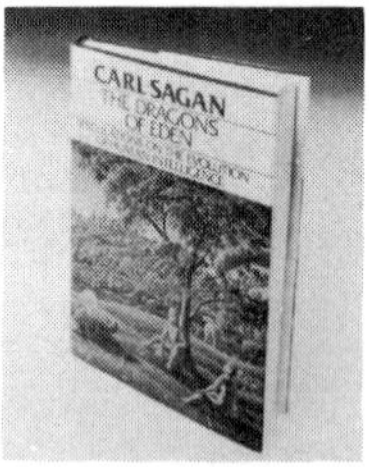
CARL SAGAN
THE DRAGONS OF EDEN

SPORTS

B28 LEFT-HANDED TENNIS BROCHURE.
Illustrated articles by Rod Laver, Tom Gorman, and others on lefty strategy—playing against righties and lefties, changing to lefty strokes, and more. $ .50

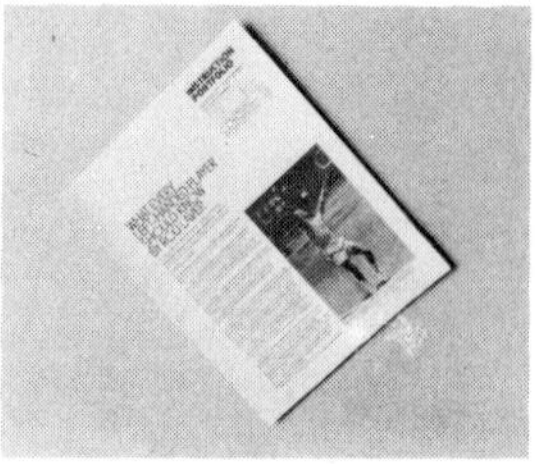

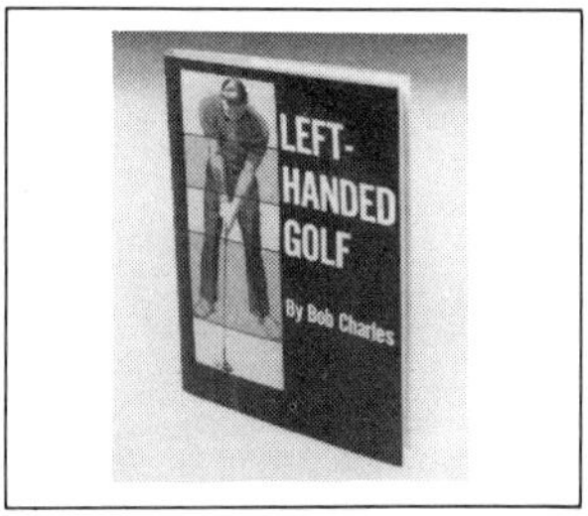
LEFT-
HANDED
GOLF
By Bob Charles

C14 LEFT-HANDED GOLF. By famous lefty New Zealander champ, Bob Charles. Includes tips on playing courses. Illustrated. $6.95

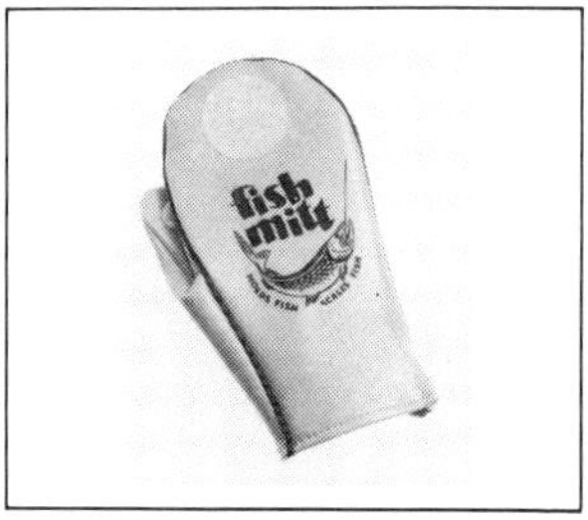
fish
mitt

F10 LEFT-HANDED FISH MITT. Reversible useful tool. Wear it on your right hand and it will hold fish for fish removal. Then put it on your left hand to scale fish. Made from durable vinyl, and it floats. $7.50

Lefty Golf Clubs

F20 Persimmon Driver w/ adjustable swingweight feature. $49.95

F21 Persimmon #2 Wood w/ adjustable swingweight feature. $49.95

F23 Laminated Driver. $39.95

F24 Laminated #2 Wood. $39.95

F25 Laminated #6 Wood. $39.95

F26 Laminated #7 Wood. $39.95

F27 Laminated #8 Wood. $39.95

F28 Laminated #9 Wood. $39.95

Specify "men's" or "women's" and also specify your choice of shaft stiffness: "regular" or "stiff." FOR COMPLETE TECHNICAL DETAILS ON THESE FINE CLUBS, DROP US A LINE.

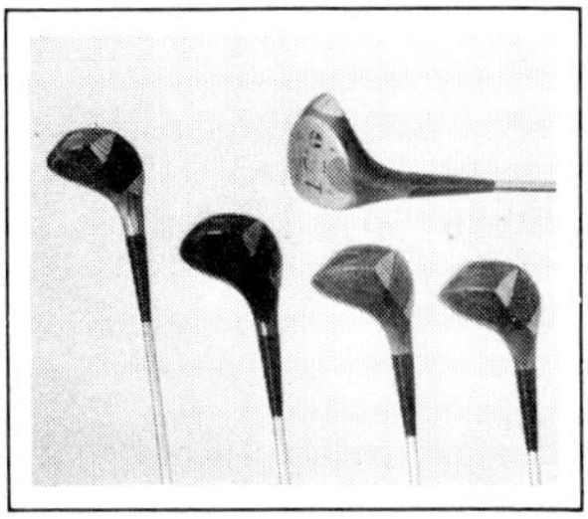

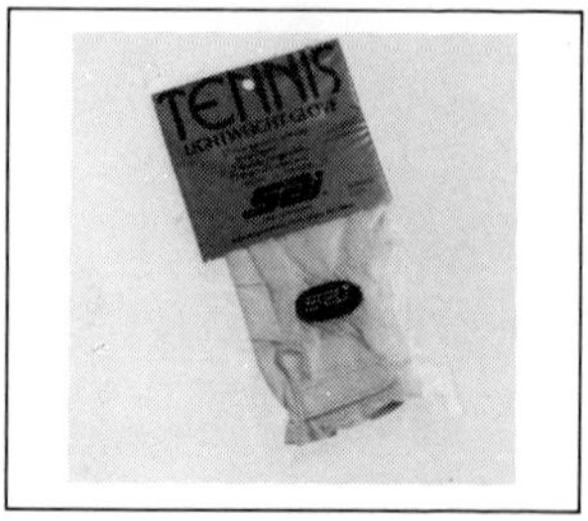
TENNIS

M01 LEFTY TENNIS GLOVE. Strong, but thin palm to retain "feel." Specify full or half finger, ladies, men's, child's. Sizes S,M,L. $5.95

LEFTY PRIDE PRODUCTS

In a recent interview, the world-famous cultural anthropologist, Margaret Mead, was asked if, after a lifetime of study, she saw any strong similarities in the cultures of different peoples throughout the world. "Everybody," she replied, "of course needs food, drink, rest, and a sense of dignity." A sense of dignity: what a nice way to say what we are really all about. The everyday life of a lefty is not fraught with peril over food, drink, or rest, but a lefty's dignity is constantly in danger, because the right-handed world forces him to do things in an unnatural and clumsy way.

In preceding sections, we have dealt with functional, physical problems and their solutions. However, years of experience have taught us that decorative solutions are every bit as important to lefty dignity and pride. With that in mind, we have developed a series of products that tell the world that lefties are really something special.

A01 LEFT-HANDED FINE DIAMOND PIN.
Jewelled flowers of diamond and gold. The flow of petal and stem is designed to flatter the right shoulder (where your lefty lady prefers her pin). The back closing is custom made to open and close easy with the left hand (no more poking extra holes and tearing dresses). 18K yellow gold setting. 39 full cut diamonds, totalling 2¼ carats. What better way to tell your lefty you love her! $5,000.00

A51   LEFTY MUGS.
Series of charming, colorfully decorated ceramic mugs with lefty themes. Show and tell others how proud you are.

A51A Mod colors and design. Says: "Lefthand Drinkers Unite, Southpaws are Beautiful." $4.50

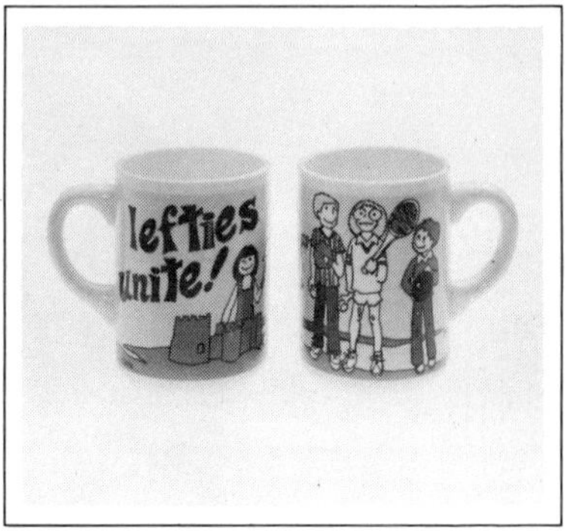
lefties
unite!

A51C Lots of lefty kids surrounding a righty kid. Says: "Lefties Unite." Great for kids. $4.50

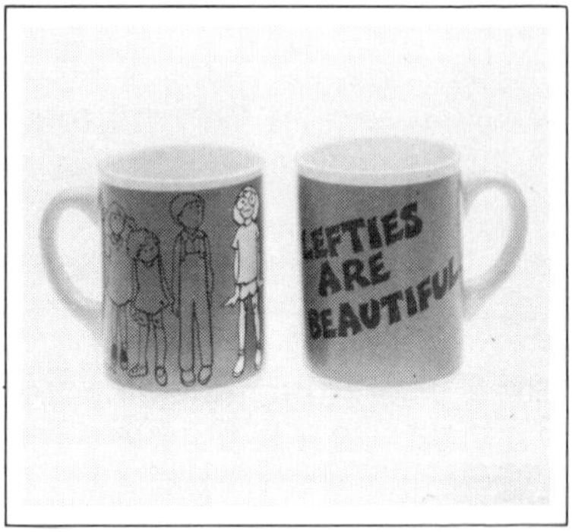
LEFTIES
ARE
BEAUTIFUL

A51D Charming lefty girl being admired by righties. White on soft blue background. Says: "Lefties are Beautiful." $4.50

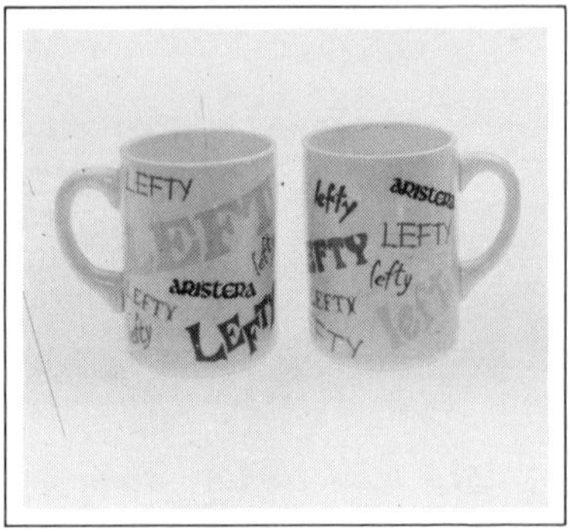
LEFTY
ARISTERA
lefty
LEFTY
lefty

A51E White background, with word "Lefty" printed in many writing styles and colors. Great for office! $4.50
Take advantage of our special offer. Any 4 for only $15.95

E01 BUMPER STICKER
(luggage sticker, briefcase, bicycle, etc.). Bright green on white background. Attractive design says "Love a Lefty" on durable vinyl. $ .75

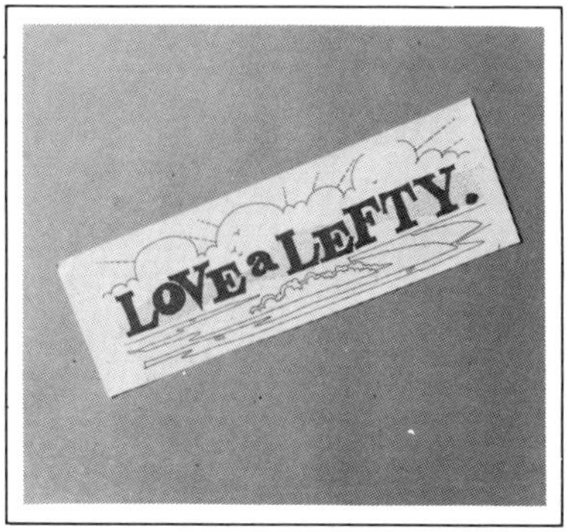
LOVE a LEFTY.

E02 LEFTY IRON-ON PATCH.
3". Bright blue letters and decoration on white background. Attractive lettering says "Lefty." $1.25

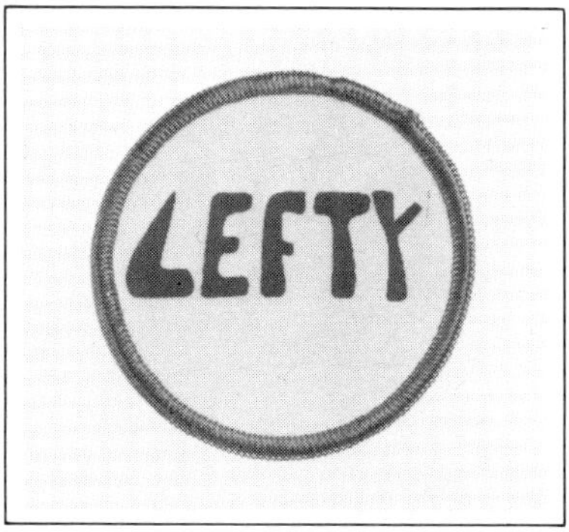
LEFTY

E50 BUTTON.
Says: "Kiss me, I'm left-handed." 3". Black letters on bright red background. Fastens in back lefty style! Fun for all. $ .75

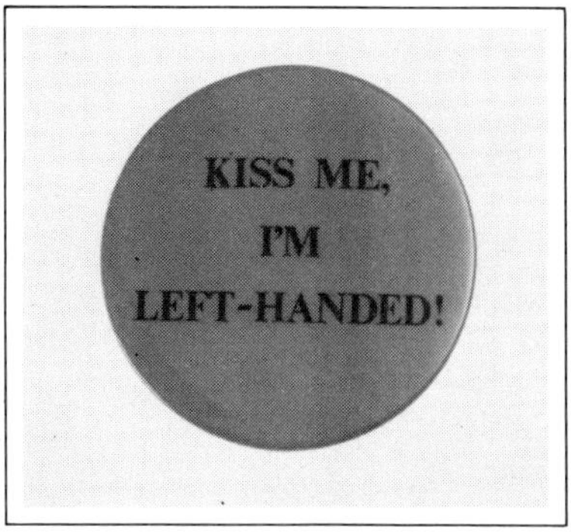
KISS ME,
I'M
LEFT-HANDED!

E60 T-SHIRT SERIES. Finest quality 100% cotton, machine washable and dryable. **MAXIMUM 1% SHRINKAGE** guarantee, and will not fade when cared for according to the label instructions. **Specify size:** Adult, Male/Female—S,M,L,XL, or Children's—S,M,L. If you are not sure of the size, specify age and ordinary clothing size, we'll take it from there.

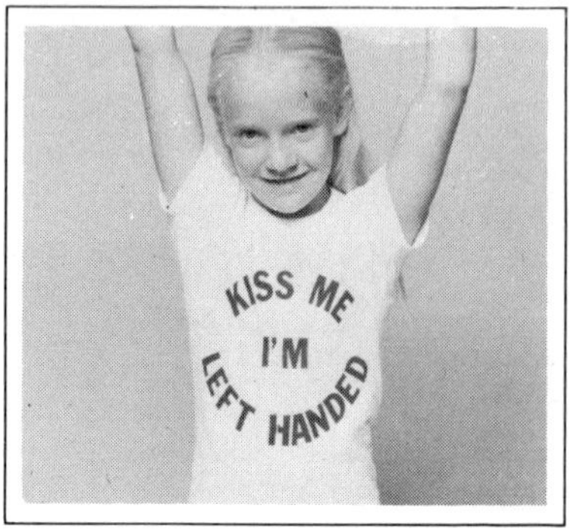
KISS ME
I'M
LEFT HANDED

E60A. White w/black letters: KISS ME, I'M LEFTHANDED. $4.95

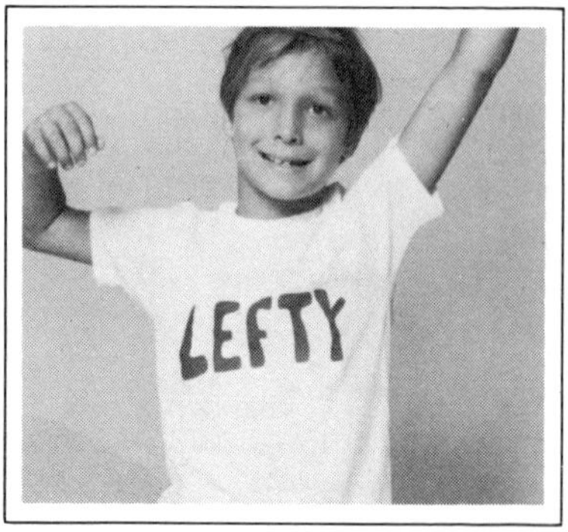
LEFTY

E60B. White w/black letters: LEFTY. $4.95

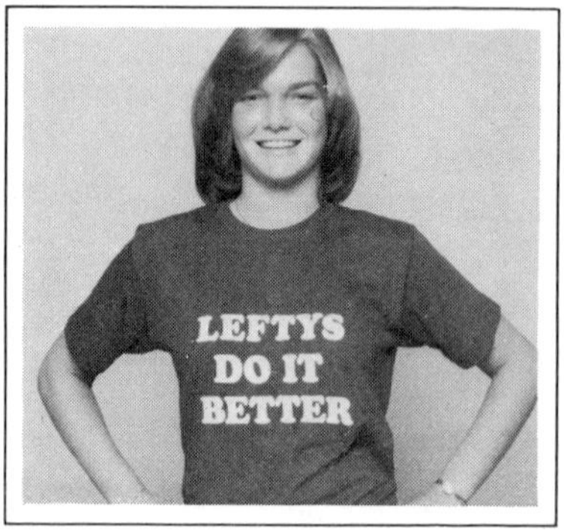
LEFTYS
DO IT
BETTER

E60C. Blue w/white letters: LEFTYS DO IT BETTER. $5.95

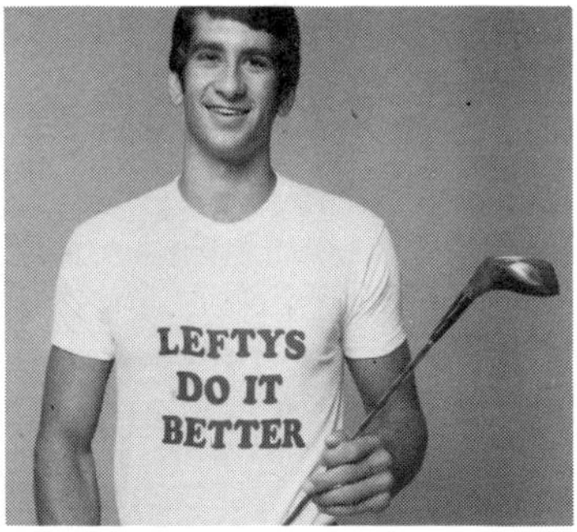
LEFTYS
DO IT
BETTER

E60D. White w/black letters: LEFTYS DO IT BETTER. $4.95

Take advantage of our special offer. Any 3 for only $13.95

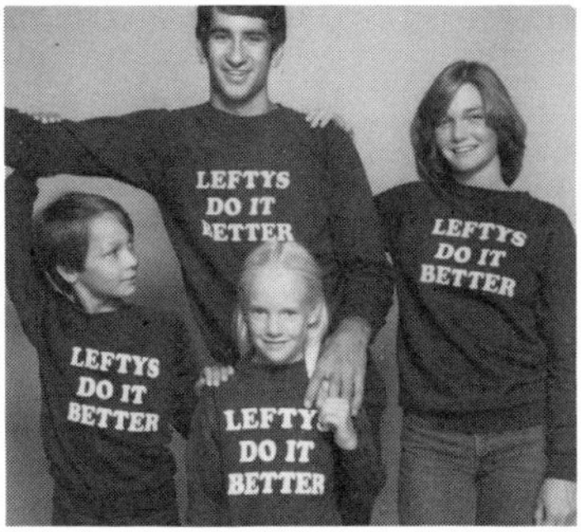
LEFTYS
DO IT
BETTER

E61A LEFTY SWEAT SHIRT. Finest quality 94% cotton/6% synthetic blend. Machine washable and dryable. **MAXIMUM 1% SHRINKAGE** guarantee, and will not fade when cared for according to the label instructions. **Specify size:** Adult Male/Female—S,M,L,XL, or children's—S,M,L. If you are not sure of the size, specify age and ordinary clothing size, we'll take it from there. Blue w/white letters: LEFTYS DO IT BETTER.

Adults $10.95 Children $9.95

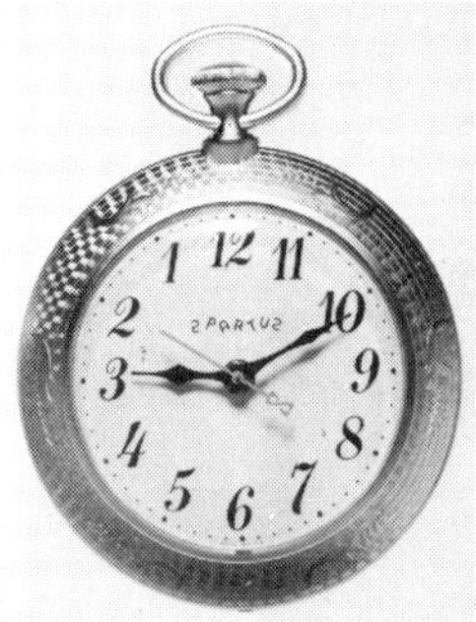

H10 COUNTERCLOCKWISE LEFTY CLOCK. Uses house current and is Underwriters Lab approved. Shaped like gigantic old-fashioned watch. Face has Gay Nineties motif. Great gift! $23.95

SOME CONCLUDING THOUGHTS

I'd like to have you keep this thought in mind: when you are pleased with our products and services, we'll know about it soon enough because you will be ordering other items and recommending us to your friends. If you are ever displeased by anything at all, let us know why. Even if the point in question seems small to you and you don't want to appear picky, it is the only way we can learn and improve our service. Let us know when you have suggestions on new products; that's how our selection grows. Finally, when you have thoughts to be included in future revisions to this catalog, send them in. Simply use the space provided on the order form, or on a separate card.

Remember: our ANY REASON GUARANTEE applies to all of the products you have read about—YOU MAY RETURN ANY ITEM FOR ANY REASON AND RECEIVE FULL PURCHASE PRICE REFUND.

I hope you have found some of the many items we carry to your liking. There is one message I would like to leave with you:

Many lefties get used to the constant stream of annoyance and insult that daily life can bring, so they think it *has* to be that way. It's not so! Awareness and self-understanding help. So does using products designed with the lefty in mind, and they're yours for the ordering.

Enjoy,

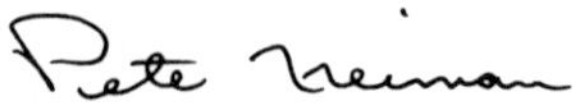

President
Aristera, The Left Hand People™

LEFTY, Write-on to THE LEFT HAND PEOPLE

Please use this space for your comments and suggestions on our products and service. If you would like us to send product information to friends, list their names and addresses here.

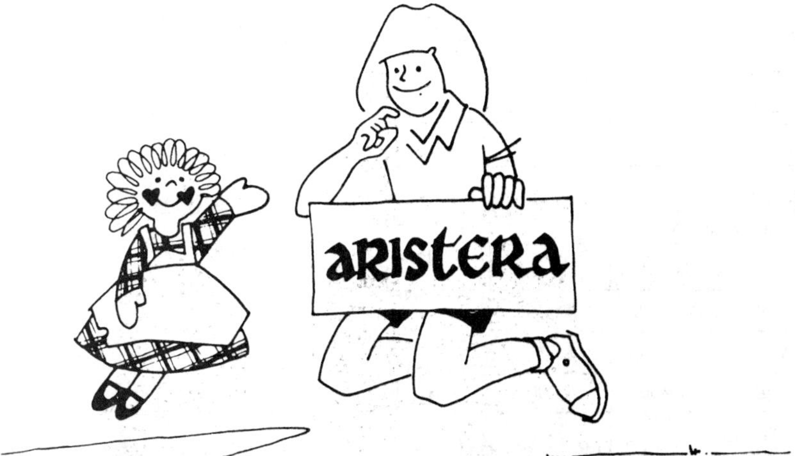
aristera

MAIL ORDER FORM

SEND ORDERS TO: Aristera, THE LEFT HAND PEOPLE,
9 Rice's Lane, Westport, Conn. 06880

Orders may be paid by cash, check, money order or VISA / MASTERCHARGE / AMERICAN EXPRESS. Sorry, no C.O.D.'s. Canadian Shipments please add $1.00 U.S.

NAME _____

ADDRESS _____

CITY _____ STATE _____ ZIP _____

ITEM NO.	QTY.	DESCRIPTION (Size, Color)	UNIT PRICE	TOTAL
		Please Be Sure to Specify Sizes When Ordering T-Shirts or Sweat Shirts.		
B				

CHARGE CARD INFORMATION
There is a $10.00 minimum on charge cards.

Which Card?_____

Acc. # _____

Expires _____

Signature _____

Merchandise Total	
Conn. Residents Add 7% Sales Tax	
Postage & Handling	
If you have a credit to your account, subtract amount	
Total Amount Enclosed	

For Postage and Handling charges, use the following table:

If Total Order Is:	Postage & Handling
$ 7.50 or under ADD	$1.45
$ 7.51 to $15.00 ADD	$1.75
$15.01 or more ADD	$1.95

If part or all of this order goes to another address, fill in below.

Name _____

Address _____

City _____ State _____ Zip _____

ITEM	
QTY.	

BONUS OFFER! For orders of $15.00 or more, you receive a free bonus of *either* E30 Tote Bag or J20 "Smart" Ruler. Specify which one on form.